Also by the editors

AFTER OVID

NEW METAMORPHOSES

AFTER OVID

NEW METAMORPHOSES

EDITED BY

MICHAEL HOFMANN

AND JAMES LASDUN

Farrar, Straus and Giroux

NEW YORK

Library of Congress Cataloging-in-Publication Data
After Ovid : new metamorphoses / edited by Michael Hofmann and James
Lasdun.—1st American ed.
p. cm.
1. Mythology, Classical—Poetry. 2. Ovid, 43 B.C.-17 or 18 A.D.—
Parodies, imitations, etc. 3. English poetry—20th century.
4. Metamorphosis—Poetry. I. Hofmann, Michael.
II. Lasdun, James.
PR195.M8A35 1995 821'.91408015—dc20 94-14358 CIP

Contents

Introduction

This book contains as many incidents, passages, characters from Ovid's *Metamorphoses* as we were able to find takers for in a year and a half, done into English by some forty poets from Britain, Ireland, America, Australia and New Zealand. There is nothing in it that was not written specially for it.

The idea arose out of our own interests as writers and readers, though, as is sometimes the way with these things, it has already begun to look a little like an idea 'whose time has come'. Ovid is once again enjoying a boom; so too is the notion of poetic translation. New Ovids are available by Allen Mandelbaum and David Slavitt. Golding's version (famously praised by Pound as the most beautiful book in the language, and out of print for most of this century) is at last being reissued by Penguin. A book in a sense complementary to this one—an anthology of historic versions of Ovid—is being edited by Charles Tomlinson, and there is a spate of new books coming out from critics and classicists.

There are many reasons for Ovid's renewed appeal. Such qualities as his mischief and cleverness, his deliberate use of shock—not always relished in the past—are contemporary values. Then, too, the stories have direct, obvious and powerful affinities with contemporary reality. They offer a mythical key to most of the more extreme forms of human behaviour and suffering, especially ones we think of as peculiarly modern: holocaust, plague, sexual harassment, rape, incest, seduction, pollution, sex-change, suicide, hetero- and homosexual love, torture, war, child-battering, depression and intoxication form the bulk of the themes. The stories are highly dramatic, proceeding with a kind of psychological perfect pitch from the natural to the supernatural, and delivering their emotional climaxes largely by means of brilliant visual effects of physical transformation. As Calvino noted, there are distinct cinematic qualities:

The *Metamorphoses* are above all the poem of rapidity. Everything has to happen at high speed, strike the imagination; every image has to overlap another image, come into focus, and then vanish. This is the principle of the cinema: each line, like each frame, must be full of visual stimuli in motion. The abhorrence of the vacuum dominates both space and time. For page after page all verbs are in the present, so that everything is happening before our eyes; events pursue each other, and anything distant is rejected. When Ovid wishes to change pace, the first thing he does is to change not the tense of the verbs but the person.*

The translator of the Loeb *Metamorphoses*, Frank Justus Miller, wrote:

Among later English poets we find a tendency to objectify the myths, to rationalize them, to philosophize upon them, draw lessons from them, and even burlesque them.

However unwittingly, we followed the methods adumbrated in these two quotations. For a change of pace, we changed our personnel. We invited each contributor 'to translate, reinterpret, reflect on or completely re-imagine the narratives', and got the full gamut. Without prescribing how, we wanted an Ovid remade, made new.

Perhaps aptly, it was a project that underwent metamorphoses of its own before arriving at this final form. By definition it resisted close control. Along the way we decided to invite only poets (dropping an earlier idea of including fiction writers); to divide the book into self-contained narrative sections of anything from ten lines to ten pages; and to dispense with Ovid's division of the whole into individual books, while preserving his general running order as far as possible. As the project relaxed into fulfilment, we minded less about omission and came to see reduplication as a positive virtue. It wasn't until our final deadline came, at the end of 1993, that we saw how long our book was going to be, how many poets we had, what sort of a metamorphosis they had worked.

Ovid's structure is not merely like a Russian doll, one story inside another inside another, it is like a snake pit, in which a pretty indeterminable number of snakes are devouring and being devoured by one another. Sometimes the central figure is the hero of a story, sometimes its narrator, cunningly telling a story that bears on his or her own. We loosened these bonds, did away with these overt complexities of inter-relatedness, leaving it to our readers to make the connections. In place

* *The Uses of Literature*, translated by Patrick Creagh. San Diego: Harcourt Brace Jovanovich, 1986.

of the unbroken song, the 'perpetuum . . . carmen' Ovid promises in the fourth line of the original, we offer the more modern, casual satisfactions of montage, repetition, obliquity, sampling, channel hopping. In addition to presenting Ovid to a contemporary audience, it was always our sense that this book would stand as a kind of anthology of contemporary poetic practice. To the extent that it does, it reveals—at the very least—a spectacular heterodoxy.

There are many poets we might have asked but didn't, even should have asked but didn't, and quite a few whom we did ask but who wouldn't or couldn't participate: among them Ai, Joseph Brodsky, Christopher Logue, Adrienne Rich and Derek Walcott. Overwhelmingly, though, the poets we asked, agreed, often enthusiastically (though that was sometimes the last we heard of them). For several months our post was transformed. This beats writing, we both thought.

If we can thank a few people, then perhaps first those poets who defeated or resisted our attempts to match them up with stories—a really invidious sort of casting; you be a pig, you sleep with your brother, you take on a double rape (often random, almost worse when they weren't) —by choosing for themselves, and thereby bringing an element of anarchy into the project. We'd like to thank our most prolific contributor, Ted Hughes, who offered a selection of three stories, to our delight did them all, and a fourth as well; and our most frequent one, Michael Longley, who kept coming back for more—or with more. It is apt that they open and close the book. To all of our contributors alike we owe gratitude for allowing our plans to distract them for an interval from their own. We are grateful to the *London Review of Books* for acting as unofficial house organ to our book. And thanks finally to our editors—Jonathan Galassi at FSG and Christopher Reid at Faber—for their enthusiasm and encouragement.

MICHAEL HOFMANN

JAMES LASDUN

New York, February 1994

AFTER OVID

NEW METAMORPHOSES

Creation/Four Ages/Flood

TED HUGHES

Now I am ready to tell how bodies are changed
Into different bodies.

I call on the supernatural powers
Who first invented
These transmogrifications
In the stuff of life.
You did it for your own amusement.
Descend again, be pleased to reanimate
This revival of those marvels.
Reveal, now, exactly
How they were performed
From the beginning
Up to this very moment.

Before sea or land, before even sky
Which contains all,
Nature wore only one mask—
Since called Chaos.
A huge agglomeration of upset.
A bolus of everything—but
As if aborted.
And the total arsenal of entropy
Already at war within it.

No sun showed one thing to another,
No moon
Played her phases in heaven,
No earth
Spun in empty air on her own magnet,

No ocean
Basked or roamed on the long beaches.

Land, sea, air, were all there
But not to be trodden, or swum in.
Air was simply darkness.
Everything fluid or vapour, form formless.
Each thing hostile
To every other thing: at every point
Hot fought cold, moist dry, soft hard, and the weightless
Resisted weight.

God, or some other artist as resourceful,
Started to sort it out.
Land here, sky there,
And sea here.
Up there, the heavenly stratosphere.
Down here, the cloudy, the windy.
He gave to each its place,
Independent, gazing about freshly.
Also resonating—
Each one a harmonic of the others,
Just like the strings
That would resound, one day, in the dome of the tortoise.

The fiery aspiration that makes heaven
Took it to the top.
The air, happy to be idle,
Lay between that and the earth
Which rested at the bottom
Engorged with heavy metals,
Embraced by delicate waters.

When the ingenious one
Had gained control of the mass
And decided the cosmic divisions
He rolled earth into a ball.
Then he commanded the water to spread out flat,

To lift itself into waves
According to the whim of the wind,
And to hurl itself at the land's edges.
He conjured springs to rise and be manifest,
Deep and gloomy ponds,
Flashing delicious lakes.
He educated
Headstrong electrifying rivers
To observe their banks—and to pour
Part of their delight into earth's dark
And to donate the remainder to ocean
Swelling the uproar on shores.

Then he instructed the plains
How to roll sweetly to the horizon.
He directed the valleys
To go deep.
And the mountains to rear up
Humping their backs.

Everywhere he taught
The tree its leaf.

Having made a pattern in heaven—
Two zones to the left, two to the right
And a fifth zone, fierier, between—
So did the Wisdom
Divide the earth's orb with the same:
A middle zone uninhabitable
Under the fire,
The outermost two zones beneath deep snow,
And between them, two temperate zones
Alternating cold and heat.

Air hung over the earth
By just so much heavier than fire
As water is lighter than earth.
There the Creator deployed cloud,

Thunder to awe the hearts of men,
And winds
To polish the bolt and the lightning.

Yet he forbade the winds
To use the air as they pleased.
Even now, as they are, within their wards,
These madhouse brothers, fighting each other,
All but shake the globe to pieces.

The East is given to Eurus—
Arabia, Persia, all that the morning star
Sees from the Himalayas.
Zephyr lives in the sunset.
Far to the North, beyond Scythia,
Beneath the Great Bear, Boreas
Bristles and turns.
Opposite, in the South,
Auster's home
Is hidden in dripping fog.

Over them all
Weightless, liquid, ether floats, pure,
Purged of every earthly taint.

Hardly had he, the wise one, ordered all this
Than the stars
Clogged before in the dark huddle of Chaos
Settled glittering into their positions.

And now to bring quick life
Into every corner
He gave the bright ground of heaven
To the gods, the stars and the planets.
To the fish he gave the waters.
To beasts the earth, to birds the air.

Nothing was any closer to the gods
Than these humble beings,
None with ampler mind,
None with a will masterful and able
To rule all the others.

Till man came.
Either the Maker
Conceiving a holier revision
Of what he had already created
Sculpted man from his own ectoplasm,
Or earth
Being such a new precipitate
Of the etheric heaven
Cradled in its dust unearthly crystals.

Then Prometheus
Gathered that fiery dust and slaked it
With the pure spring water,
And rolled it under his hands,
Pounded it, thumbed it, moulded it
Into a body shaped like that of a god.

Though all the beasts
Hang their heads from horizontal backbones
And study the earth
Beneath their feet, Prometheus
Upended man into the vertical—
So to comprehend balance.
Then tipped up his chin
So to widen his outlook on heaven.

In this way the heap of all disorder
Earth
Was altered.
It was adorned with the godlike novelty
Of man.

And the first age was gold.
Without laws, without law's enforcers,
This age understood and obeyed
What had created it.
Listening deeply, man kept faith with the source.

None dreaded judgement.
For no table of crimes measured out
The degrees of torture allotted
Between dismissal and death.
No plaintiff
Prayed in panic to the tyrant's puppet.
Undefended all felt safe and were happy.

Then the great conifers
Ruffled at home on the high hills.
They had no premonition of the axe
Hurtling towards them on its parabola.
Or of the shipyards. Or of what other lands
They would glimpse from the lift of the ocean swell.
No man had crossed salt water.

Cities had not dug themselves in
Behind deep moats, guarded by towers.
No sword had bitten at its own
Reflection in the shield. No trumpets
Amplified the battle-cries
Of lions and bulls
Out through the mouth-holes in helmets.

Men needed no weapons.
Nations loved one another.

And the earth, unbroken by plough or by hoe,
Piled the table high. Mankind
Was content to gather the abundance
Of whatever ripened.
Blackberry or strawberry, mushroom or truffle,

Every kind of nut, figs, apples, cherries,
Apricots and pears, and, ankle deep,
Acorns under the tree of the Thunderer.
Spring weather, the airs of spring,
All year long brought blossom.
The unworked earth
Whitened beneath the bowed wealth of the corn.
Rivers of milk mingled with rivers of nectar.
And out of the black oak oozed amber honey.

After Jove had castrated Saturn,
Under the new reign the Age of Silver—
(Lower than the Gold, but better
Than the coming age of Brass)—
Fell into four seasons.

Now, as never before,
All colour burnt out of it, the air
Wavered into flame. Or icicles
Strummed in the wind that made them.
Not in a cave, not in a half-snug thicket,
Not behind a windbreak of wattles,
For the first time
Man crouched under a roof, at a fire.
Now every single grain
Had to be planted
By hand, in a furrow
That had been opened in earth by groaning oxen.

After this, third in order,
The Age of Brass
Brought a brazen people,
Souls fashioned on the same anvil
As the blades their hands snatched up
Before they cooled. But still
Mankind listened deeply
To the harmony of the whole creation,
And aligned

Every action to the greater order
And not
To the blind opportunity of the moment.

Last comes the Age of Iron.
And the day of Evil dawns.
Modesty
Truth
Loyalty
Go up like a mist—a morning sigh off a graveyard.

Snares, tricks, plots come hurrying
Out of their dens in the atom.
Violence is an extrapolation
Of the cutting edge
Into the orbit of the smile.
Now comes the love of gain—a new god
Made out of the shadow
Of all the others. A god who peers
Grinning from the roots of the eye-teeth.

Now sails bulged and the cordage cracked
In winds that still bewildered the pilots.
And the long trunks of trees
That had never shifted in their lives
From some mountain fastness
Leapt in their coffins
From wavetop to wavetop
Then out over the rim of the unknown.

Meanwhile the ground, formerly free to all
As the air or sunlight,
Was portioned by surveyors into patches,
Between boundary markers, fences, ditches.
Earth's natural plenty no longer sufficed.
Man tore open the earth, and rummaged in her bowels.
Precious ores the Creator had concealed

As close to hell as possible
Were dug up—a new drug
For the criminal. So now iron comes
With its cruel ideas. And gold
With crueller. Combined, they bring war—
War, insatiable for the one,
With bloody hands employing the other.
Now man lives only by plunder. The guest
Is booty for the host. The bride's father,
Her heirloom, is a windfall piggybank
For the groom to shatter. Brothers
Who ought to love each other
Prefer to loathe. The husband longs
To bury his wife and she him.
Stepmothers, for the sake of their stepsons,
Study poisons. And sons grieve
Over their father's obdurate good health.
The inward ear, attuned to the Creator,
Is underfoot like a dog's turd. Astraea,
The Virgin
Of Justice—the incorruptible
Last of the immortals—
Abandons the blood-fouled earth.

But not even heaven was safe.
Now came the turn of the giants.
Excited by this human novelty—freedom
From the long sight and hard knowledge
Of divine wisdom—they coveted
The very throne of Jove. They piled to the stars
A ramp of mountains, then climbed it.

Almighty Jove
Mobilized his thunderbolts. That salvo
Blew the top off Olympus,
Toppled the shattered
Pelion off Ossa

And dumped it
Over the giants.
They were squashed like ripe grapes.

Mother Earth, soaked with their blood,
Puddled her own clay in it and created
Out of the sludgy mortar new offspring
Formed like men.

These hybrids were deaf
To the intelligence of heaven. They were revolted
By the very idea
Of a god and sought only
How to kill each other.
The paternal bent for murder alone bred true.

Observing all this from his height
Jove groaned. It reminded him
Of what Lycaon had done at a banquet.
As he thought of that such a fury
Took hold of the Father of Heaven
It amazed even himself.

Then the gods jump to obey
His heaven-shaking summons to council.
The lesser gods come hurrying
From all over the Universe.
They stream along the Milky Way, their highway,
To the Thunderer's throne
Between the wide-open halls, ablaze with lights,
Where the chief gods
Are housed in the precincts of Jove's palace
At the very summit of heaven
As in their own shrines.

When the gods had taken their seats
Jove loomed over them,
Leaning on his ivory sceptre.

He swung back his mane
With a movement that jolted
The sea, the continents and heaven itself.
His lips curled from the flame of his anger
As he spoke: 'When the giants
Whose arms came in hundreds,
Each of them a separate sea-monster,
Reached for heaven, I was less angered.
Those creatures were dreadful
But they were few—one family.
Many venomous branches, a single root.
They could be plucked out with a single jerk.
But now, to the ocean's furthest shore,
I have to root out, family by family,
Mankind's teeming millions.
Yet I swear
By the rivers that run through the underworld
This is what I shall do.
You think heaven is safe?
We have a population of demi-gods,
Satyrs, nymphs, fauns, the playful
Spirits of wild places,
Astral entities who loiter about.
When we denied these the freedom of heaven
We compensated them
With their grottoes and crags, their woods and their well-springs,
Their dells and knolls. In all these sanctuaries
We should protect them.
Imagine their fears
Since the uncontrollable Lycaon
Plotted against me, and attempted
To do away with me—Jove, King of Heaven,
Whose right hand
Rests among thunderheads and whose left
Sways the divine assembly?'

The gods roared their outrage.
They shouted

For instant correction
Of this madman.
Just as when those gangsters
Tried to wash out Rome's name
With Caesar's blood
Mankind recoiled stunned
As at the world's ending and
The very air hallucinated horrors.

O Augustus, just as you see now
The solicitude of all your people
So did the Father of Heaven
Survey that of the gods.

Just so, too, the majesty of Jove
Quieted heaven with a gesture.
'This crime', he told them,
'Has been fully punished. What it was
And how I dealt with it, now let me tell you.
The corruption of mankind
Rose to my nostrils, here in heaven,
As a stench of putrid flesh.
Seeking better news of the species
I left Olympus, and in the shape of a man
Walked the earth.
If I were to recount, in every detail,
How man has distorted himself
With his greed, his lies, his indifference,
The end of time, I think,
Would overtake the reckoning.
Alerted as I was
Still I was unprepared for what I found.
I had crossed Maenalus—
The asylum of lions and bears.
I had passed Cyllene
And the shaggy heights and gorges
Of freezing Lycaeus.

At nightfall
I came to the unwelcoming hearth
Of the Arcadian king.
I revealed, with a sign,
The presence of a god.
But when the whole court
Fell to the ground and worshipped,
King Lycaon laughed.
He called them credulous fools.
"The simplest of experiments", he snarled,
"Will show us whether this guest of ours
Is the mighty god he wants us to think him
Or some common rascal. Then the truth
Will stare us all in the face."

Lycaon's demonstration
Was to be the shortest of cuts.
He planned to come to my bed, where I slept that night,
And kill me.
But he could not resist embellishing
His little test
With one introductory refinement.

Among his prisoners, as a hostage,
Was a Molossian. Lycaon picked this man,
Cut his throat, bled him, butchered him
And while the joints still twitched
Put some to bob in a stew, the rest to roast.

The moment
He set this mess in front of me on the table
I acted.
With a single thunderbolt
I collapsed his palazzo.
One bang, and the whole pile came down
Onto the household idols and jujus
That this monster favoured.

The lightning had gone clean through Lycaon.
His hair was in spikes.
Somehow he staggered
Half-lifted by the whumping blast
Out of the explosion.
Then out across open ground
Trying to scream. As he tried
To force out screams
He retched howls.
His screams
Were vomited howls.
Trying to shout to his people
He heard only his own howls.
Froth lathered his lips.
Then the blood-thirst, natural to him,
Went insane.
From that moment
The Lord of Arcadia
Runs after sheep. He rejoices
As a wolf starved almost to death
In a frenzy of slaughter.

His royal garments, formerly half his wealth,
Are a pelt of jagged hair.
His arms are lean legs.
He has become a wolf.

But still his humanity clings to him
And suffers in him.
The same grizzly mane,
The same black-ringed, yellow,
Pinpoint-pupilled eyes, the same
Demented grimace. His every movement possessed
By the same unappeasable self.

So one house is destroyed.
But one only. Through the whole earth
Every roof

Is the den of a Lycaon.
In this universal new religion
All are fanatics—suckled
Not by the sweet wisdom of heaven
But by a wolf. All adore, all worship
Greed, cruelty, the Lycaon
In themselves. All are guilty.
Therefore all must be punished. I have spoken.'

As he ended, one half the gods
Added their boom of approval
To his rage. The other deepened it
With solid and silent assent.
But all were quietly appalled
To imagine mankind annihilated.
What would heaven do
With a globeful of empty temples?
Altars attended
Only by spiders. Was earth's beauty
Henceforth to be judged
Solely by the single-minded
Palates of wild beasts
And returned to the worm
Because man had failed?

God comforted the gods.
If everything were left to him, he promised,
He could produce a new humanity—
Different from the first model and far
More prudently fashioned.

So now Jove bent his mind to the deletion
Of these living generations. He pondered
Mass electrocution by lightning.
But what if the atoms ignited?
What if a single ladder of flame
Rushing up through the elements
Reduced heaven to an afterglow? Moreover,

God as he was, he knew
That earth's and heaven's lease for survival
Is nothing more than a lease.
That both must fall together—
The globe and its brightness combined
Like a tear
Or a single bead of sweat—
Into the bottomless fires of the first, last forge.

Afraid that he might just touch off that future
With such weapons, forged in that same smithy,
He reversed his ideas.
He dipped his anger in the thought of water.
Rain, downpour, deluge, flood—these
Could drown the human race, and be harmless.

In a moment he had withdrawn the blast
That fixes the Northern ice.
He tethered the parching winds
Off mountains and out of deserts
That bare the glaring blue and crack lips.
He gave the whole earth to the South wind.
Deep into the East and into the West
Vast wings of water opened.
One thunderhead filled heaven,
Feathered with darkness, bringing darkness,
From below the Equator.
The face of this South wind, as he came,
Boiled with squalling tempest.
Beard and hair were a whorl of hurricanes.
He dragged whole oceans up, like a peacock shawl.
And as he drubbed and wrung the clouds
Between skyfuls of fist, quaking the earth
Shocks of thunder dumped the floods.
Juno's messenger, the rainbow,
Sweeping from earth to heaven, topped up the darkness.
Every crop was flattened. The farmer's year
Of labour dissolved as he wept.

But still there was not water enough in heaven
To quench the fury of Jove.
So Neptune, his brother, god of the seas,
Brought up tidal waves,
And assembled every river
There in the bottom of ocean
And ordered them to open their aquifers,
Ignoring all confines.
The rivers raced back to their sources
And erupted.
Neptune himself harpooned the earth, with his trident.
Convulsed, it quaked open
Crevasse beneath crevasse
Disgorging the subterranean waters.

Now flood heaps out over flood.
Orchards, crops, herds, farms are scooped up
And sucked down
Into the overland maelstrom.
Temples and their statues liquefy
Kneeling into the swirls.
Whatever roof or spire or turret
Resists the rip of currents
Goes under the climbing levels.
Till earth and sea seem one—a single sea
Without a shore.
A few crowds are squeezed on diminishing islets
Of hill-tops.
Men are rowing in circles aimlessly, crazed
Where they ploughed straight furrows or steered wagons.
One pitches a sail over corn.
Another steers his keel
Over his own chimney.
One catches a fish in the top of an elm.
Anchors drag over grazing
Or get a grip under vine roots.
Where lean goats craned for brown tufts
Fat seals gambol over and under each other.

The Nereids roam astounded
Through submerged gardens,
Swim in silent wonder into kitchens,
Touch the eyes of marble busts that gaze
Down long avenues, under the wavering light.

Dolphins churn through copses.
Hunting their prey into oak trees, they shake out acorns
That sink slowly.
Wolves manage awhile,
Resting their heads on drowned and floating sheep.
Lions ride exhausted horses. Tigers
Try to mount foundering bullocks.
The strong stag's fine long legs,
Tiring weedier, tangle in undercurrents.
The wild boar, the poor swimmer, soon goes under.
Even his faithful heavy defenders,
The lightning flash and thunderbolt of his tusks,
Have joined the weight against him.
Birds grow tired of the air.
The ocean, with nowhere else to go,
Makes its bed in the hills,
Pulling its coverlet over bare summits.

While starvation picks off the survivors

Drowned mankind, imploring limbs outspread,
Floats like a plague of dead frogs.

Flood

JORIE GRAHAM

1

So in the cave of the winds he prisoned the north wind.

(no, it's too heavy, besides, how shall I put it)

And the north wind and the west wind and such others as

(sometimes the mood of a moment, sometimes an almond tree)

as cause the clouds of the sky to flee, and he turned loose

(oh empty cupboards, waiting for sleep, sleep)

turned the southerly loose and the southerly came

(we are far into the cave of seem, uneven rain, how

shall I put it) came out streaming, with drenched wings

dripping, and pitch black (how the Prince would laugh)

darkness veiling his terrible

(in those days and how his stories)

countenance, his beard

(but look out this window) (how solemn you are!)

heavy with rain, his locks a torrent, mists his chaplet,

and his wings (and you slept) and his linens and his other garments

running with rain . . .

2

Now his wide hands squeeze together the wide low-hanging

clouds. Crash and rumble. Cloudbursts. Rainbow.

We are so happy in our way of life.

Thunder fills the apartment like news then is re-
                                 placed—
(because it's true?)

and then the doorbell rang—

and then the rainbow's there, light drawing water from
                              the teeming mud
and sucking it up into the cloud again. Nothing

remains. (To say how pleased). Although a rumbling's

drawn across the sky. And tiny insuck where the cigarette
                                    is lit.
And hums. And clicks. And lower tones . . . Well that will do. So in the end
                                          something
remains? But what? The crops aren't spared. The farmer

prays. See him now in his dark kitchen at the
                         seeping
end of day—back bent at prayer—right there at the heart

of events—the hollow inside him

swinging, dusty, Yahweh's gamble, Jove's quick

rage, and a sudden breeze at the very end now of
                              this day
lifting the curtains, lifting the tiny beaded seam of sun
                              in them—
something that won't rub off it you should wish

to take it in your hands. (Oh take it in your hands). Then it is night.

3

Next day, blue skies. Below, blue mud with sky in it.

Above, blue sky with its mud hidden—

mud opening its seams, mud slackening the hard em-
                              bankments—
thinning them—silt—chalk—as if the whole thing should be
                              sky—field-walls

dissolving—hedgerows stringy streams—roots splayed—

roots rotted off—white slush—and cell walls, slush—

and the honeycombing masonry that separates and breeds, slush—

whole hillsides of thread-thin ash-white roots exposed,

all running downhill, gleaming, watery,

slipping their threaded, knotted

source, and the stems
     are set free,
and the leafy ex-
     tensions of rootline, the sun's
outermost meta-
     morphoses, light's outstretched

nailtip, light's beckonings, light's green
    in-chatters with sun

now glazed-down
    darkly, drawn down over the newly-exposed scree—
wilty, syrupy—

    —(as if the whole world must dissolve again)—

scummy, sleek—all the stubby quickenings of difference now

crushed back into one inky mottling, dank—the world
                  a sudden ripening
over rock and then, in the rush, the world just shiny
                rock again—

4

Oh let the river horses run wild as ever they would.

Their hooves: the rocks amid the deep roots loosening.

Their heavy breathing: the acceleration; rivulets
                  venting in sudden
loose spots—whitewaters, incurlings—

foam and tossing of manes over bedrock, tossing
        where the muscle of taproot snaps—

gleaming withers where rock-lichens are stripped off, where
                  difference is sanded

off . . .
    And they obeyed, running.

And the earth opened for them.

And orchards are swept away, grain stores and cattle.

And men and houses, bridges, (temples), (shrines with

holy fires)—

5

An anchor drags the still-green meadow. A dog

barks, or is it a piece of cornice floating by. A feature. A
                              distinction . . . Do you wish
                        to pick it up?
A living cow floats among the floating carcasses.

Dogs come swimming with curious wonders.

(It is an honor) (this carrying what is being said)

Sun fingers down, weakening, to the city-park
                              below;
row-houses; fencing. Schools turning abruptly, catching
                              the light,
the private life, what is the private life, what is it
                        that is *nobody's*
                        business
through this glassless display-case,

through this length of hallway holding corridors of water?

Bass dive through the woods.

A wolf swims frantic by the floating lamb.

A living deer and a doll—dress wide with floating—

are borne along—

the wild pig finds all his strength useless—

is there impatience now? there is no impatience—

the deer cannot outspeed the current—

the wind tries to billow the surface of water
but finds itself slowed to a thick ripple—

birds fly low looking for someplace to land—
one tumbles, exhausted, into the current—

the wings are turned again and again by waters—
frothings, suctions: they change shape
                              slightly
but do not vary . . .

Those are not hills, nor are they caves—
(the deep has buried the hills)—

Those are not depths nor are they walls—
(the deep has taken the downtown in)—

Those are not pearls nor are they eyes—
(like a bored salesgirl, current gnaws the banks)—
and all whom the water has spared will now
                              begin
to starve.

Deucalion and Pyrrha

CHRISTOPHER REID

                    Only
two survived the flood.
We are not of their blood,
springing instead from the bones
of the great mother: stones,
what have you—rocks, boulders—
hurled over their shoulders
by that pious pair
and becoming people, where
and as they hit the ground.
Since when, we have always found
something hard, ungracious,
        obdurate in our natures,
a strain of the very earth
that gave us our abrupt birth;
but a pang, too, at the back
of the mind: a loss . . . a lack . . .

Give: Daphne and Apollo

ALICE FULTON

A Foreplay

I'll entertain questions before the stellar estrus
    commences: if you want.
        But since it's you I depend on
        to change the lines to living

ground and figure, I'd rather have you
find the answers on your own. Remember how

        music was aroused in the old technology?
The stylus vibrated, shaking a crystal in its head,
    and the groove culled this trembling.
The stylus made electrons fly
    from the atom, climb a wire through
the crystal to the gate. There

    the slight current was amplified,
bridling the large—

    and vinyl gave
rise to sonatas, rise to bop.

    This gives the odd god
and hound dog, dolphin and electron,
    the novation and the moment
of change. Since the truly new
looks truly wrong at first,

    it gives the sublime and grotesque,
hoping you'll receive them kindly,

hoping for the best—newness
    being not so much a truth

as it is emotion.
Can you feel for the dark

    matter, background
lines of lace or brides? Will you
        receive the hybridized and recombined,
the downsized and the amplified?

The greenery and systemic herbicide:
    the laurel wreath.

    As estrogenic effects collect—
in heat and blur and curve—will you receive
        the minus and the plus,
the—not to mention, but I must—

    then some inbetween?

1 / Mail

What they had in common went beyond the I'm-cool-are-you-cool
handshakes and passion
for bloodsport. From forever, they were too alike to get along.
She was incidental
at first, a bit player in their boy-god drama—which began
when both
of them claimed 'My Way' as his song. Both were superheroes
in the action-
figure category. Both were fond of cherry bombs. But their
biggest
similarity was this: deep down they were profoundly
superficial.
This kinship prevented them from seeing anything but difference

in each other's
style. Phoebus Apollo favored snapbrim hats, alligator shoes

and sharkskin
suits from Sy Devore's Hollywood men's store. In battle,
stripped to the mail
he wore beneath and crowned with light, he glowed like a
refinery
turning crude into product, roaring Doric columns of flame. 'I
make everything
and make it into everything else,' he liked to claim. He took
pride
in how cultured he was, a musician of pansexual magnitude with
his suave
ballads of desire. His friends—who had to listen to him

brag
about the last rival he'd skewered against the high F
cymbal,
the broad he'd slammed against a two-way mirror—called him
Your Eminence
to his face and The Monster privately. Of course, he had
his own line
of designer products. His PR people washed the death out of
his image
and got him onto cookies and air fresheners, among other things.
He could lip-sync
in ten languages and was globally marketed as The General Voice
Swoon Pope
and Chairman of the Board, though provincial

to the bone,
he called any place outside Parnassus 'Darke County,
Ohio'.
Jove was 'the Big J'; a good time 'a little hey-hey'.
Himself he dubbed
The Republic Thunderbolt; Cupid, The Bell Airacobra
Venus Flytrap

and Fluttering Pharmacy of Love—which seems unfair since
Phoebus
gained his own fame as a healer by prescribing Chivas
Regal.

Cupid's skin was napped with floral fuzz and exhibited
a creamish structure,
like mayonnaise but more dense. He resembled a flesh-eating
botanical.
Yet that gosh-darn boyish charm of his made it hard
to credit
the two-shot derringer glued to his thigh. He'd aim
at chandeliers
and light switches, fire into his Ferrari if the battery went
dead.
But his bullets always ricocheted, striking someone
in the heart.
He sleepwalked and needed looking after.
Phoebus
considered him a frivolous child, carny spirit, gyrating
primitive
and part of nature, which only amused the little god.
'I fly
because I take myself so lightly,' he'd smile. You'd hear

a helicopter drone.
Then this vision appeared, frosted with glittering filaments
from the soles
of his feet to his little mauve wings—whose nectar-secreting
glands
kept him fat and sticky. Or else it was the fried peanut
butter and banana
sandwiches he always craved. Apollo ate nothing
but pasta
with a dab of porpoise sauce. He despised Cupid for dressing
in a blouse
slashed to the waist and a tiny gold-lined cape from Nudie's
Rodeo Tailors.

For the mixed metaphor of his jumpsuit that flared to wedding
bells white
as a pitcher plant's. Apollo was still exulting over

his recent easy-
listening hit when he happened on Cupid's opening
at the Vegas Hilton.
'What right hast thou to sing "My Way", thou imbecilic Fanny
Farmer midge larva,
thou sewer-water-spitting gargoyle, rednecked bladderwort,
dirtbag, greasedome
and alleged immortal of a boy,' Apollo fumed. 'Do thou be
content
to smite the teen queens with your rancid aphrodisiac and cover
not
my swinging tunes. "My Way" is my song; with it I have
penetrated
the pestilential coils of rock and roll that smothered
the charts
with plague-engendering form, for which I received
the Presidential
Medal of Freedom and a Ph.D. To think I did all that, and not
like Thor,
and not like Zorro. Oh no. I did much more—' And Cupid
interrupted, 'Your way

is all head and no heart. I'll get you cock-cold, you technical
reptile.
I'll neuter you, dude. I'll delete-obscene-verb your brains
till they bleed.
When the King's feeling vengeful, this old world sees stars.
He holds
his crossbow like a Fender guitar. He makes
a hybrid
from a dog and a god. Their hearts go WOOF when he shoots
his wad.'
So saying he twitched his wings and flew directly to The Aladdin
Hotel in Vegas.

There he pressed two records of opposite effect: one fostered
an autonomy unravished
as the winter wind's; one, an imperial grunt, made the listener
wish
to dominate and call it love. The first, unlabeled, went to
Daphne,
who adored the wilderness between territory and names.
The other,
on the SUN label, was mailed off to Apollo who mistook it for a
tribute
from his star cult and was pierced. Cupid hadn't forgotten how
Apollo
thee-and-thoued him. He gave the God of Truth new words.
'Well, strike me pink,
what a fix I'm in,' Phoebus found himself saying. 'I'm belching
like the hound
that got into the gin. Pard' me for trying to give trees
a hug.
I'm in love. Umm! I might throw up.' Daphne,
meanwhile,
began stockpiling weapons, studying strategic arms in friendly
competition

with Apollo's sister Phoebe. Like Phoebus, Phoebe loved
a fast bird,
a good gun and same-sex parties. Each member of her all-girl
band
had a signature whistle the others used as summons.
Daphne
swirled with them through the forest, neither mortal nor
immortal,
but a creature inbetween. Her beauty was mutable.
Take
her hair, redly restless as a vixen's or dolphin-
silver
from minute to minute. Frothing like white water it was
channeled
by a single ribbon so tributaries escaped and trickled down her

face. A dangerous
draw followed in her wake. Downstream, her current seemed
friendly, ready
to negotiate and give. Upstream you had to fight the deep
meanders of her
thought. Many wanted her and how to coax a river daughter from

her chosen
bed became the question. She would not
be dammed.
Hissing, camouflaged by a palladium haze, she'd bounce
sound
off distant objects to predict their motion, shape, and place.
Echolocation
is what she used to navigate, traveling up to one hundred miles
a day.
Her sonar let her see right through opacities: read
the entrails
coiled inside the trees. The skeletons of beasts looked
lightning-struck
to her: locked in the moment when the bones glow
through
the skin, and given three outwardly kind people, she could find
the one
whose heart was sour. But her gift for visualizing the inner

chambers
of words was most impressive. She'd tell of *wedlock*'s wall
that was a shroud
of pink, its wall that was a picket fence, the one of chainlink
and one
that was all strings. While Apollo hardened with love for her,
Daphne
stripped the euphemism from the pith. *Love* was nothing
but a suite
of polished steel: mirrors breeding mirrors in successions
of forever, his
name amplified through sons of sons and coats of arms,

her limbs
spidering, her mind changed to moss and symbol, a trousseau of
fumed wood,
the scent of perforations as his relief rose above her
smoky field.

2 / *The Lines Are Wound on Wooden Bobbins,*
Formerly Bones

A daughter like the openwork of lace == between
          the raised motif

          the field, formed by lines
of thread called brides, shies back

      in order to let shine. The design
          from negative space

      shapes its figured river == suns
star == the white thorns == sperm == and patterns

verb the ground. Through the brides'
          or pearl-ties'

airy flesh of net, wayward electrons
          spin

      with their absent grace and
          windowing

      through the opaque == the dense
omissions crystallize the lack

      that's lace. She is to be that
          yin of linen

that dissolves
under vision's dominion == be the ground

of silk that's burned away with lye ==
                    the bride.

3 / Take: A Roman Wedding

. . . She, hating the whitethorn wedding torch as if it were a thing of evil . . .
                    I, 483

It was lit at the bride's hearth while she played
        at resistance, clinging to her mother's arms
                    in lovely terror: let me be chaste! Her part
                    in the mock rape was to beg.

A parade formed to take her

                            to his house.
        What festive obscenities.

                            She listened.
        Pipes and timbrels.

                            Venereal hymns.
        Thigh or breast?

                            What wild X is seized?

The groom tossed walnuts like a soiled confetti.
        A boy ran with the torch. A portent.
                            If it soared: children.
                            If it flickered: a jinx.
The orange veil hid the right of her glance.

                    It was a drastic enhancer, the fire
thrashing round the whitethorn core. It was hair
            grabbed by heaven, coronary-colored. Spires
    from Apollo's crown, it gored the night. Spermed

a tail like a comet's

        and metastasized

to her new hearth.

        Became

  a tossed bouquet.

        Became

heavier on consummation,

      when the smoke was weighed.

The remnants, a negative

      of baby's breath,

were divided by the guests.

Once upon a bride there was a time.

Between twelve and twenty. But a minor

   all her life. Once—no often, every war—

 she was taken by force, as spoils, as lifting

     her over

the threshold remembers.

         And the whitethorn still grows.

The organza branches

    of today's hybrids—though susceptible

     to fireblight—

   are entirely free

of nettles.

4 / Undoing

Take:

her wish to be chaste. And exist in violent cloister.

To be unravished as a prime

of rainbow—a red or blue

unsplittable

through any prism. Take

the as-it-is-as-it-is—
the script. Use two hands and twist.

If you're a virgin, what are you doing
running around the woods, getting raped?
Curving every which way
in nonconjugal space.
Don't you know the best manners are the least
obtrusive? Your presence pursues its own undoing.
Just asking for it: Just use two hands and twist.
As it is as it is: your femaleness naturally
says take. Says this rape has your name on it.
Your beauty provokes
its own dominion, whose no can never mean no.
How does that one go? TO OPEN
SCRIPT PUSH DOWN WHILE TURNING

While spinning her negative charge
she has—like a wave—no single location.
If pushed through a slot, her velocity
compounds. Take
a hue outside the spectrum,
an unchromatic octave
higher than the eye can see,
a singular—unravished shade. Name it she.
Her color, name it nevergreen.

As to her bareness and her glance,
he wants to array it in flame
sandals and flame veil, a white tunic
with a double-knotted sash.
Give it an iron ring.
Put on its high-heeled sneakers—put
its wig-hat on its head. Its dress
of a fine smooth textile
made in filament and staple form
from wood pulp
solutions extruded through

spinnerets
and solidified in baths or air.

He wants to part her hair with a lance.
To make her rayon likeness,
evergreen as glance. His composite
new improved her. Cast her
in fibers of modified wood pulp found in
butcher linen or tire cords.

Prestige involves accumulation.
His desire to collect her
assumes a type—and others of the.
A kind—not one of a.
A whole forest to be had.
Let arrows stand for probabilities.

If he bored in close he'd find her bare
charge higher than it seemed == an infinite
beneath an infinite shield == an infinite
that can't be split
by modifying in the middle.
Neither soft nor hard, bright nor
dull, she traveled fast and had no given.
The more he tied her down as to position
the less he knew of her
momentum. Always transported, always elsewhere
before he == *who was she*

to tabernacle in the woods?
Place a minus sign in front of it.
Haze her
escape. TO OPEN—LINE UP ARROW
ON SCRIPT AND VICTIM
PUSH SCRIPT UP WITH THUMB.

No matter how many of her he gathered together
in his name, she would not

be the natural he could cultivate.
Though cast as lady or grotesque,
as hectic membrane in the flesh,
she would be neither-nor.

5 / *Splice: A Grotesque*

(DAPHNE)

From un-image, a form sexes itself to presence, gaining ground
        and traction, draws itself
                              together, erect
in chlorophyll surround and flapping like the sun
                    up close, like a raptor, becomes
the popular god, the can-you-imagine rose and thorn
        under wraps, the classical glance of him
            visible for an instant as he
ripples between stills, trying to settle
        into his perfection like a nest,
                       trying to light,
to don his marble artifice, flare into
            his precise foreverness.

      Pulse. What use is that to him. Go figure.
        Given the heavens, he's the stellar,
not the black bridle between stars. He's the type
      on white, he's text. He's monarch, please,
he's god. The impressive == living end.
Though luminous matter is less than one percent
        of the whole
required for closure, though foreground
was an afterthought, he's the great attractor the field falls
        on its knees before. Go figure.
When he speaks his subjects
        want to listen up—be liked
           by such exclusionary beauty. Oh please.

And trying to introduce himself and light,
    trying to settle his perfection like a net,
to produce his sovereignty, I.D., he's taken aback
      by what's recorded
in the velour ground of his voice,

        and I witness, riveted,
as he naturalizes, looking surprised,
as his suede bass mutates—
             'I pray thee'
    blurring to 'Hey Baby',
            'Ah me!'
  to 'No sirree!'
      Witness as he yields his definition,
        shrinks, grows
        jowls, pants, bays,

      drools like a hound, all his torch
pulled downward—is transposed
    from lyric plea to what my mother called dog minor,
and his scent—the exsanguinated scent
    of godly flesh—the rank smell
    of hound begins to foul it,
surprising him, still clinging to eminence
      as he naturalizes, pure splice,

hymn to hound—raptor to roadrunner—blurring
          before firming up—
     as witness, I am midwife
    to the pulse, the composite
      pelt and feathers, the nascent maybe
      monstrous innovation of
a god with a gift in his teeth,
    who bows
until his mouth is thrust between his legs,
      wags his tail and stammers—
'Hey Talltits, I ain't stealing what you own'—
     and I realize he thinks that—

'Just a bit-a bit-a honey
        that you have on loan'—what I'm living in,
            the dark matter of myself—
                        is his.

*   *   *   *   *

My mother's thistled lyrics
        whiptail into mind.
I witnessed as she sang herself
        into top billing at The Apollo,

upstaging everyone with her seminal presence,
    using her unretractable claws
        to form and deform oracles, her songs
        to open cyclone fencing,
        gnaw through planks and deadfalls,

    voice to drag a live
trap chained to massive logs, climb the walls
and splinter bars—saw the mainstream

    call her marginal, though she was a star
        in her own field, big enough
        to give the spotlight to her backup band,
        say 'Play your solo, honey,'

        before shouting her hit,
the one that didn't cross over
            but made the King rich
                in his cover version,
        say—'Now I'm gone

to do my *own* self song' and sing
        the lyrics he'd omitted—
    'Want to steal my power, want to steal
my soul—you ain't lookin' for a woman,
    you is lookin' for a hole—'

lines that stem through me
as he tries to urge her from my head—
             to drown, femme, wrestle—
what verb—god—
             yes, god her saurian voice into the ground.

                    *   *   *   *   *

Give again the legend
that her tongue bore a charge
and could be used as a support,
             how she'd eat her own skin to keep elusive,
             how she was something

        nothing could stalk,
give her unscannable—knowing

             hunters wait for the quarry to step forward
                   she'd stay withdrawn, the planet—
                        Big Mama, Gaea, Earth Goddess—
                           underneath their stance,

give her command to turn—turn—

the story of her death,
             how she was embodied as the python—dragonlady—
till something struck her—clamped on—
        her voice was bathed in exaltation—
till something clamped onto her like—Apollo

        who'd built a ring of thorns
                   around her as she slept—
        so that trying to escape, she was impaled
on the barbed crown—Apollo—

        who crept within the mantic embers of her death
                   to steal the oracle—boasting
that he'd killed the monster—this god of light

who wants me
to love or pity him, I cannot
tell, he's that grotesque == god who threatens

'You can lose a bay leaf
from a laurel tree—lose-a lose-a your lunch, dear—
but you'll never lose me, uh-uh-uh—
no sirree,' defends
'Doggone it, Bachelor-Girl, I'm Phoebus not a fibber,
so be a Natural-Girl,
not a hairy Ladies-Libber,' sweet-talks
'Inky-Dink Nymphie, don't say toodle-loo—
I'm Apollo, not some moron out to oo-
oo-oogle you,' wheedles
Yo! Miss Daphne, doncha say amscray—
How 'bout it baby,
wanna hear "My Way"?' flatters
'You're a real sharp article,
and I want you for my steady—
don't be a frigid particle,
say all right already,' a god who chatters
'Listen, little lady, you're mighty pretty scenery
but if you don't get friendly,
Pops will turn you into greenery—'
snapping his fingers, rhyming 'bimbo' with 'limbo'—

because light is a bully,
shoving everything it touches—
existing to figure
pattern and scheme
rather than let things rest

in the nocturnal recessed bed ==

*   *   *   *   *

He told her he was high-class,
but she could see through that.

Chanting her labels—
     Backbeat Baytone Broom Arhoolie
     Peacock Pointer Solid Smoke Buddah,

her albums—'Jail' through 'Stronger Than Dirt',

    I skirt the limits of detectability,
become the knit and backbone of immersion
    against which everything exists—

become the skin under the gooseflesh—in her words
    —I lense, I nevergreen—

    I dedicate myself to reticence,
        and blending ahead
of the high-octane god—
        whistling by above his range—
  'My heart is barking' I hear him pant
  and have to laugh—I hear the thing

she always said when I attended
  her immense voice in my head—

she, whose buried teeth could sprout an army,
    (do girl)
who lived in her luxurious revolving hut,
    (do girl oh)
her agon of corrosion and sowing,
    (do remember me)
chemise of moss and rust,

      I hear her grandly in my head—
commanding honey—I want you to. She wants me to

turn.

   Into what, I always wondered—

Turn.   Into the huge nocturnal
              noose around the Virgo cluster?

Turn.   She never finished the sentence—

              till now—I hear her asking me at last to

Turn—her—loose—

6 / Supernal

Apollo pulls a cloud back like a foreskin
              on the sky that is his body.
His laserscope will amplify
           the available starlight,
zero in on the nymph
    in her stealth boots
           that leave no helpful scent.
Daphne—who is graphite,
    darkling, carbon as the crow—

                is out of breath.
If only the stars would tire,
    she might find cover.
If only they would empathize.
    But who will help a person
    on the wrong side of a god?
All largo, she turns to face Apollo.

Though she expected him
           to wear blaze orange, supernal
as the sun, he tracked her down in camo-
    skin, which 'disappears in a wide variety of terrains'.
He owns every pattern in the catalogue.
    After considering *Hollywood Treestand*
           ('all a nymph sees is limbs')

and *Universal Bark*,
         ('a look most guys relate to')
he chose a suit of *Laurel Ghost*,
printed with a 3-D photo of the forest,
            which 'makes you so invisible
        only the oaks will know you're there'.
Even his arrow's shaft is camo.
    Only his ammo jackets gleam
           like lipstick tubes.

Is it any wonder, when his wheel-bow
    has been torture-tested
to a million flexes,
           his capsicum fogger
fires clouds that can cause blindness,
       his subminiature heat detector
finds the game by the game's own radiation,
       and the tiny boom mike in his ear
lets him hear a nymph's grunt from 200 yards—

any wonder—when the ad said
            'Put this baby to your eye
and see if she's worth harvesting' and
    'See the hairs on a nymph's ass,
        up close and personal'—
that he turns the housing, gets her
    on the zeroing grid,
and now his snout at her fair loins doth snatch?

Who can she turn to, the monastic, almost
        abstract Daphne?
The stars are tireless. She decides—
    no, winds up—
    pleading, in extremis, with her father:

            '. . . I am not like
them, indefatigable, but if you are a god you will

not discriminate against me. Yet—if you may fulfill
        none but prayers dressed
        as gifts in return for your gifts—disregard the request.'

That's when her father makes her
                        into nature, the famous green novation.
And Daphne—who was hunter and electron—
                        is done with aspiration.
Did you see it coming? You're a better man than she.
                        With no one to turn to—
                                she turns to a tree.

7 / Turn: A Version

(TREE)

She'll get out of this one somehow. Someday she'll break
our engagement
with a wraparound roll-off or axel full twist
dismount,
followed by a blast of wind that puts an end to this grotesque
togetherness.
'The suckers love a weird wedding'. That's what her father said
when she called
on him for help. Forget Io and Arachne. He was thinking
Teenage Mutant
Ninja Turtles. Roger Rabbit, Mr. Ed. People get a kick out of
ambivalent
betrothals and collisions full of give. Flowers that
remodel
themselves to look like bees are nice, but the scientist whose
atoms get commingled
with a fly's might be my favorite. 'Help me! Help me!'
I can identify.

Yes, it tamed her, being changed into a tree,
but consider

what went on in me. I had a moment's prodrome, the premonition
before seizure or disease.
I heard voices—'Hi, I'll be your server for tonight' and
'Can I see your I.D.?'
Then, in a migraine-pink epiphany, I knew I was
a tree. 'It'
turned to 'me'. As Daphne sank, ensorcelled by my thorazine
hush, I heard
the whitewater rush of what I was. To you it might have seemed
'the tree heaved upwards
and twisted like a sleeper in brown sheets' but the process
felt plaid
to me, like madras bleeding—color stabbing color

as it never does
in nature. Heavenly hurt. I recognized the presence
of design.
She moved through my zen nap like a queen—
yes Your Deviance—
riding up like a skirt, abrading my chambers and rays till she
crowned. Oh,
she was a sensation. It was not consensual, let me tell you.
Whose 'no'
can never mean 'no'? I was opened and she was spiralbound
as nature/culture,
the great divide, broke down. 'I'd like you to meet Daphne,'

said the River God, her father.
Please—what's the word for opposite of—'like to meet
Daphne?'
What's the word for what is doing ground loops, flying
the great circle course,
uppity, aspiring, reaching 100 knots in me?
Daphne apparently
did not know her position. I experienced tremendous
interference.
She said she was changing to nighttime frequency: it was dark
as a casket

where she was headed. 'What is your position?' I transmitted.
'Partly cloudy,'
she responded. 'What is your position?' I asked again.
'Approximate.
Whistling now. Please take bearing on us and report . . .'
'We are unable . . .
it is impractical to take a bearing on your voice,' I said.
'We are circling . . .
must be on you but cannot see you,' she came through. I felt
the lead tickle of her

ribbons, her heavy mittens with a trigger finger stitched in,
her nuclear skirts
and coppertoed fauve boots. She was carrying an old Kentucky
rifle, a Pioneer
Drift Indicator and a 'very orange kite'.
'I'm dead meat,'
she said, and then—'I am not friendly'. That must be when
I freaked. I drooled
amber as trees do when they're hurt. I salivated
resin blond
as baby shampoo, lactated the bud-gold of
extra-virgin
olive oil to trap the pathogen, Daphne, in a gown of sap
for good.
What's the phrase that means how fast the growth layers spin?
Velocity of domain.
I circled her in no time, head to toe, in a million
wedding rings.

My first emotion happened to be revulsion: an ungreen, sour
cramp
as Daphne shrank—'oh, baby,' he kept saying—from Apollo's
colonizing kiss.
Of course, he liked her better as a tree. 'Girls *are* trees'
was his belief. Mediated
forms pleased him. 'If you can't find a partner, use
a wooden chair,'

he'd say. Well, every fetish tells a story. I felt her bows
and powders,
guns and arrows change to pom-poms, a cheerleader's pleated
skirt.
'As she jumps up try to pull her to the sky and slightly
forward,' he coached.
'Every beat in a yell should have a motion. Give us an A,
Give
us a P! End the yell with a good freeze.' Then her power
mount
pike through—she tried to get away—become a shoulder
straddle to cradle—
as 'Nice Save!'—I caught her in her grave. I choked on
volts
of hairspray as—step-step-step-ball-
change—
she became his pep club. Pure as a
symbol,

toned, in racing trim, for her just standing still was
grim. 'Safe
in your alabaster chambers,' she'd sigh. I noticed she became
more babyish
as the centuries passed by. She couldn't walk, had no control
over her body,
and often babbled rather than talked: 'Sis-boom-bah. Doobie-
doobie-doo.
Oo boy or oo girl?' Frivolous. Gerber's gibberish.
And I
became her pacifier. She called me Mr. Crib.

Oblique grain develops after an injury—like Daphne
teething
on my rings. The growth tornadoes, polarity
breaks
and the grain departs from the ideal of straight == deviating ==
making waves
that form diverse and beautiful chambers. People find it

hard
to say which way a tree is spiraling—whether dextral or
sinistral—
and mistakes are often made. The Germans say with or against
the sun,

the English, clockwise or counter, from the on-high perspective
of the gods.
In America, the vortex is described by observers on the ground,
with much twisting
of wrists and waving of arms. But no one sees it from the
standpoint
of a tree. Oblique grain is useless for transmission
poles, plywood, or veneers,
and so a tree with it is thought abnormal: a 'monstrositat'.
But spirality
isn't a sickness or condition. Since it makes me less desirable
to commerce
and being harvested is not in my best interests, I consider it
a plus.

I had zero spiral before Daphne. I've heard the aberration
depends
on what it turns against. And every part of me has turned
against
a woman's body. The stretchmarks *she* developed are a story
in themselves.
We talked by thought which made us really close.
Others
might consider her a kvetch, but we became best friends.
I understood
because I *was* her by then, wrapped up in the electric flex
of her
ideas: I learned women were debarred from sweating and vision
seeking,
that the female was the prey of the species . . . adapted
to the egg's needs
rather than her own. When Daphne first heard this she'd begged

her father,
saying 'Feed me, also, River God,
lest by diminished vitality and abated
vigilance, I become food for crocodiles—for that quicksand
of gluttony, which is legion. It is there—close at hand—
    on either side
    of me.' He agreed but later, of course, he changed

her to a tree. To me
she was unnatural. People don't realize—'natural'
is a habit.
Once otherness gets in, a something else entirely begins.
Newness
isn't truth so much as a motion. At first, I resented her
efforts
to transcend me. It was like sleeping with a jostled beehive
in my stem, between her
vengeful 'next times' and torrential 'should-have-dones'.

I said
'You should have sought your *mother's* help when trying to
escape.'
But face it, mothers were the ones who bound their
daughters'
feet. The experts said deflate him with a spike heel or a hat
pin,
but who wears such things? Not *this* wood nymph. And he was a
god,
for Christ's sake! He had all the stellar leverage. He was a
tactician
of infinity—a god! Her mother, Gaea, was the Earth Goddess,
yes—
but she'd always pressured Daphne to major in Home Ec.
'Man produces,
woman reproduces.' Her mother took that line. 'Why can't you
be a gatherer
like all the other girls?' 'Next time I'll go for the less

embedded delicacies,' Daphne cried. 'I'll mime "little"
with my index
finger and thumb.' I'll say this: she wasn't a pleaser.
She lacked
a slave mentality, though she modeled herself on Apollo's twin
and 'modeled'
is probably too weak a word. She *did* Phoebe. She had a
Phoebe act.
It was Phoebe this and Phoebe that. She ran with Phoebe's band
and cut
quite a figure as The Little Sureshot Riverbrat, Maid of the Myth,
with a star
on her hat. She could snuff a burning candle with a bullet,
break
five eggs before they hit the ground and pierce the ace
of hearts.
All with her back to the target, while aiming in her compact.

When captured,
she kept shooting through my cambium, reaching beyond
the bodycast
of lassos I'd become, and her hand, part of her hand, her
trigger finger
I think, got slammed outside my trunk and is preserved there
in amber, an organic gem.
If brass were clear, it would resemble amber. If wood were.
Silk as flesh
kept always clothed, gold as cologne, as beer, as urine, warm
to the touch,
absorbent, *elektron* in Greek or substance of the sun, light
in the fist,

amber—collects a negative charge when rubbed. It preserves
organic tissue
very well, which might explain why Chopin handled
amber chains
before performing and Roman soldiers wore amber-studded mail as
their palladium.

I was surprised to find 200 terms for it in certain Polish
dialects.
But no word exists that is the opposite of 'like to meet
Daphne'.
The more private the wish the less likely there's a
term
for it. Did I say she's always having visions, as in ancient
versions
of the myth? She sees herself discovered, maybe

in my side,
washed out of context, or buried in blue earth. She'll tell
her story
rather than be held inside its web. There are holes—
have you noticed—
where the seams don't quite close? Daphne peers through
those gaps.
She scans the sky and plans to stare—you can almost hear her
glance—
down the air, the blank, the optical until
a face stares back.

8 / Stereo

(TREE)

A sea-pen, these mirrors, the lively gray
of oceans with the ocean's active, turnstile look.

The god, wanting to placate her, implanted these
to make the cage of me seem larger.
Now she who was so eager
for a view, a glimpse of the remembered

weather, sloshes up
against herself in silverface
on every side.

'I think that I shall never see . . .'

She seems perplexed at being her own tether.
I hear her say it is yourself you

do this to, I am like you, and wonder who
is being accused.

'If a mirror starts to fall,
let it. Never try to catch it.'
A caution

I recall as again, again,
against the self of her that he installed
she hurls herself—

     so entertainingly—

who could bear to save her.

9 / A New Release

(DAPHNE)

A voice changed to a vinyl disc, a black larynx,
spun
on the hi-fi as we called it, before light was used to
amplify
and the laser's little wand got rid of hiss. The
diamond-tipped
stylus stroked the spiral groove and guitars flared out of
reticence:
the first bars of a hit. I always wanted to hear it
again,
though it was always in my head: sticky,
invasive,

and what else in that culture was that
dark?

Easing the new release from its sleeve, I saw myself
bent
out of shape in its reflections: a night whirlpool or a
geisha's
sleek chignon, an obsidian never reached by skin
since skin
always has a warmth of blood beneath. It was a synthetic
Goodyear black,
like all records, pressed with a tread the needle traced,
threading
sound through ear and nerves and marrow. I touched its
subtle
grain sometimes wondering how music lurked in negative
space
that looked so unassuming. The marvel was—the missing
had volition.
And the spaces between tracks were a still profounder
black: darker than bitter-
sweet Nestlés, coffee ground from chicory, or Coke. Black
as it must be inside

a tree. 'Wear My Ring Around Your Neck,' the latest
hoodlum Cupid sang.
He aimed at objects and hit people, it was rumored.
His urgent nonsense—
about hound dogs, rabbits, class and lies—changed
aren't to *ain't*,
were to *was*, *anything* to *nothing*. 'Caught' was the
operative
verb. While couples jived and twisted I must have
listened
differently—as to a special pressing—with my head
against
the set. Somehow, by the last chill tingle of the cymbal
I wanted

to be the singer rather than the wearer of the ring.
To this day,
rodents gnawing at the wooden walls remind me of the rasp

of dust
before a cut. A cut. That's what we called a song.
And handsaws—
harvesting the forest in the distance where I live—
sound
like the end: the rhythmic scribble of stylus against
label
when everybody's left. Everybody's gone
to bed.
And the record turns and turns into
the night.

Io

KENNETH KOCH

Look at this lovely river maid, who bears the name of Io—
Her youthful beauty caused in Jove such ache that 'Me, oh! my, oh!'
He cried, 'she must be mine!' and when he had the maid deluded
And had some happiness with her, she as a cow concluded.
It happened this way. Jove one morning as he walked along,
Singing a sort of thissy-thatsy gay Olympian song,
Beheld a female, Io—and her beauty made him shiver—
Come running from her father's banks (her father was a river,
Inachus, a Thessalian one, who flowed through Tempe Valley—
So many lovely girls have river dads originally!
Rivers who are immortal but must flow against the odds
Being no match, in case of crisis, for the greater gods,
Such as, in this case, Jupiter, who strolling by their waters
May bring great harm because of love intended to their daughters—
And yet, and yet, you'll see when you are finished with this story
They suffer, yes, but often end up consummate with glory—
Io, I'll tell you in advance, was in this category)—
In any case, the King of Gods (as if gods needed rulers—
It's a conception both profound and worthy of preschoolers),
The King of Gods espying her, in her bodacious tresses,
Desired for to fuck with her beside the watercresses,
'Where we'll be cool,' he said, 'and you'll be safe as you are stunning—
I shall protect you—'
                    But she had already started running
And ran through Lerna Marsh and ran through Lincie's budding woods
Till Jove, impatient, brought a fog upon these neighborhoods,
A thick and foggy mist, in which the girl had trouble seeing,
And being lost was to her cost one with Eternal Being—
Which is to say, Jove had his way and pressed himself inside her
And for that portion of the day felt happy as a glider.
  However, Juno, jealous Juno, zealous brunette, looking
At so dark mist on such fair day, demanded what was cooking,

For there was not a river or a marsh or swamp around
That could be sending up such foggy substance from the ground.
'Husband!' she cried, and went around to all Olympian places
Searching for him but found him not among the bearded faces.
'Well, I suppose, what else, God knows, he's at his usual capers,
Getting a girl with the assistance of substantial vapors.
We'll put a stop to that!' she said. And, 'Mists, be on your way!'
And suddenly above the god it was translucent day.
But Jupiter had seen in time what Juno was about
And by the time she got to earth there was a kind of snout,
Well not snout really but a bovine heightened kind of nose
On Io's face and from her flattened head two horns arose;
Her arms had turned to legs—so she was well-equipped to walk
Close to the ground—her mouth could graze, and gape, but could not
    talk.
She still was white and pretty though she was a heifer now.
Juno admired her grudgingly. 'Where did you find this cow?'
She questioned. 'From what herd is she?' And Jupiter replied,
'She sprouted up here from the ground.' But Juno knew he lied.
'Darling, she's such a lovely one, I'd like her for a gift.'
'Er, well, my dear—' Jove felt some fear. And he had little shrift—
He didn't want to give his sweetheart to his nagging wife,
But also didn't want her nagging at him all his life,
Which was eternal. And it seemed so small a thing to ask—
A cow!—'Of course, all right,' he said, his face a pleasant mask,
Although inside he didn't like at all what he was doing.
    The goddess, having got the former Girl, who now was mooing,
Needed to figure out a way to keep her precious prize
Away from Jupiter. And then she thought of Argus' eyes!
One hundred eyes adorned the head of Argus. When he slept
He closed but two (I do not know what happened when he wept)—
In any case, for guardian of a woman or a cow,
No one could watch as Argus could, and his is Io now.
'Let her go out by day,' said Juno, 'let her roam around,
But when the night comes, fasten her with willows to the ground.'
Argus agreed, whose sight was such that Io he discerned
When facing her or to the side or when his back was turned.
She fed on leaves and bitter plants and muddy water drank

And oft at night to rocky ground in restless sleep she sank.
She wanted to stretch out her arms to him in supplication
But had no arms to stretch, and in no way by conversation
Could she excite his pity, but could only moo, and seem
The more a cow.
                     One day she walked beside her father's stream.
The sun was bright, the air was still, there scarcely was a zephyr—
It made the heart expand even though the heart was in a heifer.
Then, bending down her head, she looked and saw her face reflected:
What gaping jaws, what horrid horns were to her self connected!
She started back in awful fear and bolted here and there;
Her sister naiads petted her to soothe her, unaware
Of course that she was Io. (How she wanted to be one
Of the Inachus girls again, handmaidens of the sun
And wood and way and water, but those days, it seemed, were done!)
Now she was with her sisters, but she walked on hoofy feet;
Was with her father, but was dumb. He brought her grass to eat.
He, miserable, aflood with grief, had searched with no success
For Io everywhere, and did not know and could not guess
Whether she was among the Shades or if she still drew breath—
Since she was nowhere, he feared for her something worse than death.
Distracted now he feeds the pretty cow, who licks his hand.
Weeping, she longs to find some way to make him understand,
And with her hoof she traces her name IO in the sand.
(How fortunate that she was not named Thesmophoriazusa
Or Melancholy Myrtle, or Somatacalapoosa—
For by the time she wrote it out her strength would have been wasted,
Inachus have gone elsewhere, or the rising tide erased it.)
At once her father understood. 'Oh woe is me!' he cried.
'You are a cow, who were my dear, my darling, and my pride!
I hoped that you would marry soon as other maidens do
And I would have a son-in-law, and have grandchildren, too,
But now I see that it must be a bull who marries you!'
He wept. She wept. He held her close, her horns and all, and said,
'What pain it is to know your pain! I wish that I were dead!
No help to you is to be had, and all to me is futile—
Alas the Gate of Death is closed and I am an immortal!'
Now as her father made lament, Argus with eyes like stars

Removed her from those latitudes and past the Eastern bars
To where she grazed in other pastures; and he found a seat
Atop a mountain where his view of Io was complete.

Jupiter now had had enough. He didn't want the heifer
Because of Juno's jealousy so horribly to suffer.
He summoned Mercury and said, 'O nephew of the Pleiade,
Great messenger, enchanter, go, and rescue me my Naiad!'
Whereat the god took up his magic cap and wingèd shoes
And sleep-producing wand—he didn't travel without those—
And came to earth. Pretending he's a goatherd, he advances
Where Argus is, upon a syrinx playing songs and dances.
Argus was smitten by that music. 'Come and sit with me.
There's grass for goats and shade for us,' he said to Mercury.

The god agreed, and sat and played sweet notes till Argus dozed
But also stayed awake, since only half his eyes were closed—
Some of those open still kept watch, and others paid attention
To the strange reed-pipe Mercury played, which was a new invention.
When Argus asked about it, Mercury left off playing lyrics
And told him how the pipe was born: of Pan's pursuit of Syrinx,
A wood nymph, fair and much pursued, whose wish it was to be
Diana-like, a huntress, and of perfect chastity—
And when she was attired like her, and when she held her bow,
Whether or not she was Diana it was hard to know.
Many mistook her for the goddess. When she walked one morning
On the cool slopes, and in such guise, the god Pan saw her coming
And felt for her, divinely fair, his godly spirits soaring
And went to her and said to her, 'O Maiden, thou art—' Snoring!
Not Syrinx, no, but Argus, of whom the star-studded cranium
Was veiled by eyelids like the undersides of a geranium.
Could this be true? It was. So the remainder of the tale
Argus was destined not to hear—how Pan pursued the pale
And trembling hamadryad till she came to Ladon's banks
And begged to be transformed—she was, to reeds; she murmured,
      'Thanks'
Just at the moment racing Pan caught up to her and found
He held no nymph but what best grows on moist and sandy ground,
A bunch of hollow reeds. He sighed. To lose his girl was odious
But what those reeds made of his sigh was haunting and melodious.

Touched by the wonder of the reeds, enchanted by their tone,
Pan said, 'In playing, thus, on thee, my dear, we shall be one.'
The instrument of reeds forthwith retained the name of Syrinx.
Mercury meanwhile separated Argus at the larynx,
Swiping him with his curving sword, once he had made it certain,
Using his wand, each eyeball slept behind its lidded curtain.
Bounding and bouncing down the rocks, the head of Argus flies,
One single darkness in what used to be a hundred eyes.
Juno, at seeing Argus wasted and herself upstaged,
Was—how could Jove not know she would be?—totally enraged.
First, she took Argus' eyes and placed them in the peacock's tail
Where they would always shine. Then, something sharper than a nail
She set in Io's hide, a terror-causing wasp-like goad
To torture her like fury as she ran down every road
She came to, mad with pain, forgetful even of her shape,
Wishing above all other things that stinging to escape—
Poor Io, tortured out of Greece, to race through alien dust,
Her only crime for a short time to have aroused the lust
Of one who saw her not, as she ran, stumbling in her pain,
On four short legs, until she came upon the waving grain
Of the Nile Delta, then the Nile, that cuts the land in two,
And there she stopped, Great Nile, for having got as far as You,
She could no more. Upon your shore, she lifted up her face
To stars where she thought Jove might be, commanding from that place,
And by her moos and mournful moans, on bent and knobby knees,
From suffering unendurable did beg forthwith surcease.
Jove heard her then. And pleaded, with his arm about his wife,
That she permit him to give Io back her former life.
'Fear not,' he said, 'she'll be a source of grief to you no more!'
'Swear!' Juno said. And by the deadly Stygian pools he swore.
   Juno relents. And Io starts to be herself again,
Her former self that brought delight to gods as well as men.
Her mouth and eyes decrease in size, her gaping jaw deducted,
Rough hair and hide are altered, and her horns are deconstructed.
Ten fingernails appear where were two hooves, and she has hands
And shoulders, and a waist, and, now, upon two legs she stands—
She who had altered from a naiad to a bestial form
Becomes a queenly girl again, too royal for the farm,

And is completely Io (of the cow she keeps the white
And nothing more), but, standing so, she feels a sort of fright,
A fear of speaking—what if she should moo?—but has no choice
And speaks—in words! and owns once more her interrupted voice.

Now she is worshipped as a goddess, with the greatest honor,
After she gives birth to a son perhaps begot upon her
That summer day when, graceful, gay, she ran up from the river
Her father was, and stirred the lust of Jove the Thunder-Giver.

Phaeton and the Chariot of the Sun

Fragments of an Investigative Documentary

Unearthed by GLYN MAXWELL

1 / Cine

Cine, sliver of history. A few minutes
finish you off in a blare of white, and the scutter
and scutter and sigh, then the lamp on and the smiling
that something, at least, is over.

Cine, chopper of Time, mercurial
slitter, century shadowing through our light:
London's sepia scuttle, a toadstool whitens
Nevada. Colour—Zapruder.

Cine. A reel was found in a vault in a place
I happened on in the course of a search. This reel
was not—but is now—the object of that search
so it's over. Which is how

poetry works, by the way. Like cine film
it yields to the bright. Like cine film it is either
print or nothing, like cine film that nothing
is sky. Like cine film

it's made of people who run towards you and cry.

2 / Epaphus

That's him there,
late in our fragment, laughing with three friends

as he points out to our point of view some sight
we never share.

He smokes a long
sobranie it must be, brags away at a girl
who tires of him by the look and turns to us,
licks out her tongue

and wanders up,
fanning a smirk. Now even the camera fumbles
as she approaches, she's almost filling the frame—
one wet black lip

loves all. After this
Epaphus posing with one friend only. Pale,
demurring, shrugging. Phaeton. Yes, for sure!
Freeze it. Yes,

Epaphus, his friend,
now drunk, shakes him and leers. Was this the time
he told him his father wasn't his father really
and Phaeton, stunned,

backed into space?
No, this time he grins, Phaeton, lifts
a fluted glass off a tray, downs it and grins
and sets his eyes

coolly on us,
on the lens, on the future—that hungry severity
of anything lost forever is shrinking us all
to eager toddlers

blinking back
into the flicker. He finishes up another.
His mouth is forming words while we hear nothing
but flutter and tick

then our lens
fixes on him, doesn't mean to be caught up
but jams and is. A blot spreads out of the centre
and it all burns.

3 / *The Horses' Mouths: Pyrois*

Film me in silhouette. I insist. I'm not
Them prancing nags. Is that thing rolling? No?
Good. It better not be. What you got,
Rothmans? Gimme. What do you want to know?

The boy. The boy in the chariot? Oh no.
Some things I crack about, some things I don't.
You learn the worst is never long ago.
We horses live our lives in the word 'won't'

But you don't understand, you undergods.
Gimme the Bushmills. Woh, that hits the spot.
The boy in the chariot. Hell. It makes no odds.
It happened. Why? This isn't lit. Why not?

What was the story . . . somebody made him think
His father wasn't his father? Right, so he snaps
And goes and gets his way. Dies in the drink.
Talking of which . . . No, you pedalling chaps

Think you're as free as air though you're made of earth.
You got to obey your whim like a whipped horse
Flies. That boy. He thought about his birth.
He wanted it again. He ran his course.

4 / *The Spokesman of the Sun*

Good morning, I'm researching into the death
   of this boy, do you know him?

You shake your head, but don't even take a look
    at the picture—how can you tell?
Excuse me, but we know you were on duty
    the morning he came here,
so surely you can remember him, and his name,
    and his claim that he was the son—
ah, now we're getting somewhere—he was the son
    of the Lord himself?—now, sir,
that's very expensive equipment, sir, you shouldn't
    do that, sir, we have to
suspect you if you won't assist us at all
    in our enquiries. Now—
get off my foot, please, sir. Thank you. We're merely
    asking you to recall
the morning when this boy came here, we'd like
    the viewers to know exactly
how he came to be in control of equipment
    he couldn't possibly—sir,
that's not very nice that, sir—he couldn't possibly—
    several thousand lives
depended on him, and all we want to know
    is how and why they had to
because of the negligence of your organization
    die in horrific—
sir, don't point that thing—okay, we're going!
    but thank you for your help,
I don't think—okay, we're going, we're going!
    Fuck me, did you see that?
He would have used it, too. We're out of here.
    I don't know. Some day
this work is going to get me killed, I swear.

5 / The Horses' Mouths: Eous

How did you find me here?
    This is my refuge from all human voices,
    Their differences that shrivel into hisses

All indistinct, their faces
    Merged to the infinite grains of a far shore

Licked by the dog sea.
    Here on my noiseless meadow I ride alone,
    Ride, ride myself with the wind on my spine
While the fuelled and roaring Sun
    Mislays my name in the mess of his tyranny.

Talk to the others, friend.
    Find the unkempt Pyrois; Aethon, vain
    And cosseted by Man, then look for Phlegon
Anywhere where the thin
    Are all there is, and the wind is a hurled sand.

That's his gesture. Mine?
    Mine's this solitude. I've a world to tell
    But not this world. We switched your sky into Hell
And all for a human will,
    Its pride, its point, its prick. It will come again.

How did I know it was him?
    When we were torn through clouds and the East wind
    I felt no weight on my back, heard no command,
And felt no pull, no hand,
    No pilot. No escape now. Kingdom come.

Three images, that's all.
    One was his face, the boy, his face when he lost
    The reins and then his footing—that was the last
We saw of him—he must
    Presumably have gone in a fireball—

Another was how the Moon,
    Seeing us hurtle by, reminded us all
    Of the face of a mother beside a carousel,
Worrying herself ill
    As her children wave, are gone, are back too soon—

And another was afterwards.
    I lay for a good forever somewhere in a woods.
    The petrified seconds prayed, the hours wore hoods.
'You gods,' I said, 'you gods.'
    And those, I trusted, those were my final words

To men. Instead, these are . . .
    Forget Eous, leave me alone in my meadow,
    Riding myself, racing my sisterly shadow
Into the shade, where sorrow
    Wraps her and deserts me, drenched, here.

6 / Mulciber

The Palace of the Sun. Item. Gates of.
All things are made of what I say they're made of.
The heavens, earth and fire are made of silver.
The sea is made of gods. The gods however
Themselves are made of silver. This is Triton.
What do you mean 'It's Saturn'? Nothing like him.
This is Aegeon, riding on two creatures.
Whales, you reckon? Well, they got whale features
But they ain't whales. Whales are made of blubber.
Prick this skin of a bark you've silver rubber.
Besides, you enter the legend as a vandal.
That's Proteus on the left, in the right, in the middle.
Ho! He's where I say he is. His positions
Alter daily. Simplest of commissions.
Doris rides on fishback, while her daughters
Dry their hair forever, like my daughters.
Meanwhile, back on the land, the men are manly,
The beasts are beastly, the cities urban. Only,
The sky's a bit of a solo spot for the craftsman:
Virgin, Scales, Scorpion—see yours?—Bowman,
Goat and Waterman, then on this right-hand panel
More bloody Fish, Ram, Bull, Twins (mine was the model:
One son, two images, clever, eh?), then the Pincers,

Then old Laird of the Woods. Oh and manifold dancers,
All-purpose Nymphs and Shepherds. Sightsee's over.
That concludes your visit to *World of Silver.*
Fill in the yellow form in the Antechamber
If you're interested in becoming a Silver Member.
No cameras, thank you, sir. No, we don't discuss
That. We don't take questions from the Press.
There was in fact no boy and no such flight.
Research was done. Not one thing came to light.
I showed you the Silver Gate. That's what I'm for.
And now I'm showing you the silver door.

7 / The Horses' Mouths: Aethon

One minute, love.
You're looking at
The winner of
The 2.15,
3.38,
And 5 o'clock.
I haven't time.
I race, I work.

Ask what you want
But ask it fast.
The time you spend
Is time I lose,
Is time we've lost.
Aethon never
Loses, friend,
You got that? Ever.

The chariot?
The idiot boy?
I don't admit
And never shall
I lost that day.

He may have done.
He burned. So what?
His father's son.

The countries burned,
The oceans steamed,
The stinking wind
It filled my eyes.
I never dreamed
Years afterwards
I'd humble all
These thoroughbreds

Day in day out,
Year after year,
Beyond all doubt
Beyond compare,
The sight they fear,
Aethon, pride
Of any course
You humans ride.

If all the gold
That lights this room
Was melted, rolled
And stretched for me,
I should in time
Reach Heaven's Gate
And there I'd not
Be made to wait

But rode by servants
Back to where
I rode the Heavens
Once, the Sun
Would part the air
For Aethon,

Fanfared, forgiven.
Aethon.

8 / A Scientist Explains

Would he have suffered? That depends what you mean.
Would he have suffered? Lady, let me explain.

> The fire went north.
> The northern Plough,
> Too hot to bear it,
> Plunged below
> The sea; the Snake,
> Sluggish and cold,
> Was scorched to fury;
> Boötes, old
> And slow, he too
> Was stricken down,
> He too was dragged or stricken down
> When Phaeton flew.

Would he have suffered? Suffering's hard to define.
Would he have suffered? Lady, let me explain.

> He was afraid
> Of height and now
> The world he knew
> Was spread below
> And churning. West
> He'd never make,
> The wounded East
> Bled in his wake.
> He didn't know
> The horses' names,
> He'd never thought to ask their names
> And didn't now.

Would he have suffered? Would he have suffered pain?
Would he have suffered? Lady, let me explain.

He bore the worst
Of Heaven, curved
With poison, Scorpio!
Wild, he swerved
And lost the reins
And lost the flight.
The chariot set
This world alight:
The woods and streams,
The crops and towns,
The nations perished in their towns
As in their dreams.

Would he have suffered? That depends what you mean.
Would he have suffered? Lady, let me explain.

Athos, Taurus,
Helicon,
Parnassus, Cynthus,
Babylon,
Ossa, Pindus,
Caucasus,
Olympus, Libya,
Ismarus,
Rhine and Rhone
And Nile and Tiber,
Nile and even promised Tiber?
Steam on stone.

Would he have suffered? Suffering's hard to define.
Would he have suffered? Lady, let me explain.

The seas had shrunk
And all was sand,
They felt the scorch

In Netherland:
Nereus sweltered,
Neptune swore,
The Earth appealed
High Jupiter:
'I may deserve
This doom, but spare
Your Heaven itself from fire, spare
What's left to save!'

Would he have suffered? Would he have suffered pain?
Would he have suffered? Lady, let me explain.

Obviously
One shot alone,
One thunderball
From Heaven's throne,
Divided boy
From flaming car,
Made fire of him
And falling star,
A star of him
That plunged and died
In the River Eridanus, died
Far far from home.

Would he have suffered? That depends what you mean.
Would he have suffered? Lady, let me explain.

Lady?

9 / Clymene's Coda

Death was instantaneous
Death is always instantaneous.
Loss was instantaneous.
Loss is always.

10 / The Horses' Mouths: Phlegon

Get on my back. You all do in the end.
You've come some way to go the way you came,
    But shall do, all the same,
    My doubly hopping friend,
At least you ride in peace, at least you ask my name.

Where are the other three? There's no surprise.
Eous rippling aimlessly alone,
    Pyrois wrecked, Aethon?
    Neighing at blue skies,
As if his loss, our loss, was some grand race he'd won.

I work this zone. Don't have to, but I do.
I do have to, and so would you. Look now,
    The planters on the brow,
    They falter, wondering who
Wants what of them and why. They'll try to question you.

Be plain with them. It waters you with hope
That in this desert where the fire can't die
    Nor air reach to the sky,
    Somehow they grow a crop
That doesn't care it's dead, that doesn't know. Now stop,

Get off my back. Feel hotness on each sole
And howl. For this is not the word made flesh,
    This is the word made ash,
    This is the mouth made hole,
Here where the star fell, here where he got his wish.

11 / Burned

These are what we plant.
    This is what we grow.

These are what we eat.
    This is what we know:

Nobody will come
    With any more to plant.
Those who come will come
    With bags, because they want

What we have left to eat.
    This is what we turn.
This is what we pay
    From anything we earn.

These are what we plant.
    This is what we grow.
These are what we eat.
    This is what we know:

Whatever cross we pray to,
    Whatever cross we bear,
You are earthmen, you are earthmen
    And you do not care.

12 / Phaeton and the Chariot of the Sun

Into the eye of my world
    Falls, glinting, the light of my father.
Never again shall I doubt
    That the crown I can feel is intended
But for Phaeton his son,
    I, pride of the fabulous morning.
Warm in my room I await
    The procession of brightening beauties:
She at their head who will hope;
    She, fair, who will pray to no purpose;
She near the end who'll be flung
    On the cold yellow coast of the jealous;

Soft and unique at the end
       Sighs she who is fit for Phaeton.

Cold in the day I will stare
       At the clouds that have gathered for nothing,
Nothing but murmur and doubt
       At the power and pain of my coming.
Melting the solemn away.
       I, son of all light and all loving!
Where are the arrogant now?
       Where, when will they suffer Phaeton?

Hurt in the night I can hear
       Hooves, falls in the chase of my heartbeat.
I am the one who will loom
       As a tower at the end, though my wishes
Whiten the world like a star:
       Clouds, enemies, rivals, tremble!

Out of the night I will ride,
       Burning bright through the eye of my father.
Watch me until I am gone,
       Friend. Watch me forever, and after.

The Grip of Envy

J. D. MCCLATCHY

Mercury then, god of the magic wand, flew high
    Above Munychia, the land Minerva holds dear
With its gently arbored walkways and groves.
    It was festival day. Girls with flower-wreathed
Baskets carried gifts to the temple of Pallas.
    As they turned toward home, the god saw them,
And circled, as when a hawk spots the entrails
        On an altar and fears to land while the priests
Huddle around, yet does not dare to leave,
    But hovers with beating wings above the prey—
So too did Mercury glide around the Athenian hill.
    As Lucifer burns brighter than other stars,
And as the golden moon outshines Lucifer,
    So much lovelier was Herse than any of the girls
In the procession. She was the gleam in every eye.
    Struck by her beauty, the god caught fire
Mid-air, like some sling-shot stone burning up
    On its hurtling course through the clouds.
Mercury swept down, so confident in his own
    Beauty he disdained a disguise but smoothed
Back his hair and the gold edge of his cloak.
    He struck a pose, in his right hand the wand
With which he can induce or prevent sleep itself,
    And on his feet the gleaming winged sandals.

The girl's house had three bedrooms, each adorned
    With ivory and tortoiseshell. Her brother
Slept in the right one, her sister Aglauros in the left,
    And Herse herself in the room between them.
It was Aglauros who first saw the god approaching.
    She asked his name, and why he had come.

'I am he who carries my father's commands
      Through the air, the son of Jupiter himself.
Nor shall I lie about my intentions—it is for Herse
      I am here. You will prove your sister's friend,
And become the aunt of our son, if you grant me
      Your favor and help me press a lover's claim.'
Aglauros glared at him with the same cold eyes
      That had lately spied on Minerva's secrets.
She demanded gold from the god for her services
      And meanwhile forced him to leave.

At this, the warrior goddess turned her angry eyes
      On Aglauros and sighed so deeply her breastplate
Heaved with the memory that it was this same girl
      Who had profanely revealed the secret
Of the motherless son of the Lemnian god.
      And now this very girl would, for a bribe,
Play into Mercury's hands, and her sister's.
      At once Minerva sought out the cave of Envy,
Begrimed with gore, hidden in a deep valley
      Where no sun ever shines, no breeze ever stirs,
A gloomy dwelling, shrouded in dark, cold vapors.
      When she reached the cave, Minerva could not get
Past the doors, so clanged her spear against them.
      The doors creaked open, and there was Envy
Eating snakeflesh, the food that fed her venom.
      Minerva flinched at the sight, while Envy,
Leaving the half-eaten carcasses, dragged herself up.
      When she saw the goddess in her glorious armor,
She groaned, grew pale, and shriveled up.
      Her eyes are squinty, her teeth rotted; slime-green
Gall drips down her breasts, and venom from her tongue.
      Only someone's suffering makes her smile, and constant
Cares keep her from sleeping. How she loathes any man's
      Success. She gnaws at men's hearts, gnaws on her own,
Herself her own torment. In spite of her disgust,

Minerva spoke sharply: 'Here is a task for you.
Infect with your poison one of Cecrops's daughters.
      Her name is Aglauros.' Without another word
She pressed her spear to the ground and soared heavenward.

      The hag watched Minerva depart and muttered angrily
That the goddess would have her way. She took her staff,
      Thick-set with briars, and cloaked in a cloud
Set out. Wherever she walked, the flowers withered,
      Treetops were seared, and the foulness of her breath
Sickened every city, every home. At last she came to
      Athens, the capital of all wit and joy and peace.
She wept to look upon a place that was no cause for tears.
      Entering Aglauros's chamber, she did Minerva's
Bidding: she touched the girl's breast and made her heart
      A knot of thorns, then breathed her black poison
Into the girl's nostrils and through to her very bones.
      As the cause for this convulsion, she set up
Before Aglauros's eyes the image of her sister, her sister
      Happy, her sister in bed with a god, the glamour of it
Exaggerated until Aglauros ate her heart out in jealousy.
      Careworn by day, dreamwracked by night, she slowly
Wasted away, like ice melted by a flickering heat.
      The thought of Herse's good fortune burned in her
Like the flameless fire smoldering in a pile of weeds.
      She longed to die, longed to tell her stern father
Of Herse's imagined crime. Finally she sat down
      Across the threshold of her sister's room,
As if to keep the god from entering. When he did arrive
      And pleaded softly with her, she cried out: 'Enough!
I will sit here forever until I have driven you away.'
      Mercury replied, 'So shall it be.' And with a touch
Of his wand he flung open the door to the bedroom.
      Aglauros struggled to get up, but her heavy limbs
Were motionless. Her knees went rigid, a coldness spread
      To her fingertips, the blood in her veins grew pale.

As when some cancer wanders through a body with its fatal
    News, so the deadly chill crept into the girl's breast,
Choking her breath. She never called out for help,
    And if she had tried, no words could have been formed.
Her throat had turned to stone, her face a statue's face—
    Not even white, for her soul had stained it black.

Jupiter and Europa

SIMON ARMITAGE

How very like him, Jove,
the father of the skies,
to send his silver son
down on a thread of light

to drive a team of stirks
across the lower slopes
towards the sea. A girl,
Europa, walked the beach.

Then leaving in a cloud
his three-pronged fork, he went
to ground, dressed as a stot,
a bull, and allocked there

and bezzled with the herd.
His hide was snod and bruff,
a coat so suede and soft
and chamois to the touch,

and white, as if one cut
would spill a mile of milk.
His eyes were made of moon.
His horns were carved in oak.

Europa, capt and feared,
would not go near at first,
then offered to his lips
a posy fit to eat.

Jove nuzzled at her fist,
then ligged down in the sand;

in turn she smittled him
with plants, then climbed his back,

at which he sammed her up
and plodged into the tide;
on, out, until they swammed
beyond the sight of land.

With him beneath she rode
the fields of surf, above
the brine, because the sea
might gag or garble her,

or gargle in her voice.
The waves have not the taste
of wine. A girl at sea
is never flush with choice.

And where they beached, they blent.
Or where he covered her
beneath a type of tree,
that tree was evergreen.

Cadmus and the Dragon

TOM PAULIN

If Cadmus is the Age of Reason
                  —and he is
if Cadmus is the State
                  —and he is
if Cadmus is Descartes with a scalpel
                  —maybe so
then Cadmus must also
shadow Locke with his shovel
a shovel loaded with decaying sense
but always new and stainless
like the idea of rights
—rights not duties be it said
                  —yes brother

so Locke hires a surgeon barber
to make an incision
in the Earl of Shaftesbury's right side
for like a monstrous dragon
of superstition and formal piety
the suppurating cyst on the earl's liver
menaced English liberty
but the little silver tube
that Dr Locke inserted
gave one man life
and restored the nation's freedom

therefore Cadmus laid a conduit
in the body politic
which has to mean
that we're safe and secure
with Citizen Locke
—though they set spies on him

he worked
to bring ruin on the Stuarts
and plant an orange tree at the gates
of their state brothel

but if Cadmus is a subtle doctor
it also occurs to me
that Cadmus was present at a working lunch
in the Stormont Hotel
the winter of 90 or 91
—there was a civil servant on my right
and when I glanced at his left hand
a signet ring
cut with a tiny gold pentagram
was making its point quite silently
while beyond the picture window
the neoclassical gateway
the long straight drive
—it dips into the underworld
and that hollow muscly facade
were also making
much the same point
—so Cadmus is Sir Edward Carson
raising his bronze fist
against the twisty tail of Home Rule
—a theatrical gesture
he copied from James Larkin
who raised the dragon people
against their bosses

but let's say instead
that Cadmus is Willie Whitelaw
sitting at a bootshaped table
with the Spartoi
—they wear hoods
balaclava helmets
and dark glasses
—here Cyadmus

one of the hoods says
ye cannae sit in this coul chamber
wi a bare head
at a table that's shaped
like a Wellington boot
—put you a hood on
and we'll do business
for as Lévi-Strauss'd argue
Cadmus is himself the dragon
and ancestor of the Spartoi
or as it says in the Good Book
as ye sow so shall ye reap
so know ye this
Mr Kidglove Whitelaw
we're no Piltdown Planters
but the real autochthonous thing
—we're the Cruthin aye
a remnant of the ancient British people
who rose again in 98
in 1912 and . . .
ack I forget what date it was
but let Ballylumford
be our rath and fortress
we're not the 'RA
we're the 'DA
know what I mean like?
this is *Dadmus and the Cragon*
or *With the 'Da in Craigavon*

if this seems a shade slippy
what stays constant
is that our hero Cadmus
would appear to be masculine
he's all straight lines
he's rule and measure
a rigid prick
or as Carlos Williams notes
there are plenty men

whose heads resemble
nothing so much as
the head of a dick
which is how I came to see
John Cadmus III
sitting at the wheel
of his pickup truck
in a parking lot
outside a Safeway foodstore
in Tucumcari New Mexico
—he looked a tad
like Norman Schwarzkopf
the day he turned back
on the road to Baghdad

and though I spotted
—or say I spotted
his lookalike in Tucumcari
I should have changed the location
to Rockville
    Cementville
    Oilville
    Mechanicsville
for Cadmus is a grid person
who must imagine
not *amor loci*
not *dinnseanchas*
but the absolute antithesis of place
because he fears a parish dragon
some batlike mind
that's forever trying to snuff
a cosmopolitan enlightenment
—Locke's world of signs if you like

doing a steady 55
he admires all those high
blue boards along the freeway
how they say plainly

there is a rational liberty
that goes with cotton fields gumbo
and private property
this Cadmus
he'll have no truck
with the dragon of any particular place
he's dead frightened
of the monster that lives
in a cave overgrown
with branches and sally rods
—*a deep cave rich*
in hot bubbling springs
a funky cave
where the mud is edible
and tastes of tarragon

so it would seem that the monster
the Dragon Other
just has to be a fanny
—maybe *vagina dentata*
if that's your hairy fear
or the bottomless vagina
flying in the south wind
easy effortless as a windsock
infinite as language
or everything which is the case

so this monster's a giant fanny
o starry fig
o prickly
unpricked pear
o heavy moist musty warm wrinkledness
you belong in a gothic novel
—shave yourself and it's jacobin
scratchy as a cucumber leaf
else you're a barber's strop
a sea anemone
some tinker's budget

or a thatched bothie
—an extra skin so thin
it's no skin at all

—watch Cadmus shiver
as he hears a voice crying
you too will become a monster
you'll toss your bucket
into the bairns' well
and come back as fresh water

now he imagines something
dry and itchy like a desert
warm and silky like the Nile
soft black sogflaky and
sweet as a pickled walnut
or brittle like a sea potato
furred on the tideline
yes this fleshy oxymoron
is an ocean
that's all ripples and taut muscles
it nips every cock in its pincers
and leaves behind
only a sagging fence hung with raindrops
piss sweat blood mucus
all the starchgreedy jism
they stream across
this prickly bed of tears
they enter this pouch
this tuppence hapenny
creased purse
—it's a quiver of desire
an oozy whooze
or a peppery paper wasps' nest

juiced and tightswelling
this blind cave
how it haunts the knight in armour

it'll smash every lance
that jigs into it
and mangle poor Boswell
who hides behind a rock
to try on a tricky condom
made out of a pig's intestine

or maybe this dragon
is a nation under arms
not a single hero with a name
it's the body earth
that turns out turds and babies
like loaves of bread
or it's the bloody earth
that rakes its own hills
avec les crachats rouges de la mitraille
and though its soldiers
spring fully armed
from out the grassy soil
only to hack each other
down to the last five
—the remnant
we console ourselves
that because Pallas
told them to observe a ceasefire
in order that Cadmus
might build Thebes
this has to mean
that we are all born of the spirit
and not the earth
though maybe the opposite
just happens to be the case?

Creation According to Ovid

ROBERT PINSKY

In the beginning was order, a uniform
Contending: hot cold, dry wet, light dark
Evenly distributed. The only sound

A celestial humming, void of changes
(*Playing the changes*, jazz musicians say).
And then the warring elements churned forth

The mother-father Shiva or Jehovah,
The dancing god who took a hammer and smashed
The atoms apart in rage and disarranged them

Into a sun and moon, stars and elements,
Ocean and land, the vegetation and creatures—
Including even Ovid playing the changes

In his melodious verses, including even
God the creator: himself divided male
And herself female by the sundering hammer

Held prancing, one foot on earth, one lifted in air.
From heaven to earth god came to visit the bodies
Of mortals, making himself a bull, an avid

Shower, a gibbon, a lotus. And to the one
Who had his child inside her, he promised to come
In any form she named. 'Come to me naked,'

She said, 'as in heaven with your sister-wife.'
God wept, because he knew her human frame
Could not sustain that radiance, but he danced

For her and became an annihilating burst
Of light that broke her. God grieved, and from her body
He took the embryo and tearing his thigh

Sewed it up into the wound, and nine months later
Delivered the merry god whose attributes
His many titles embody: *Drunkard; Goat;*

The Twice Born—from the mother, then the father;
The Horned—because his father was a bull-god;
Sacrificed who dies and rises, and also *Slayer;*

The Orgiast and *The Tragedy Lord; The Liar;*
Breaker of Palace Walls; The Singer (all listed
In *Metamorphoses*, which Ovid burned

In manuscript because it was unfinished
When he was exiled, though other copies survived);
Disrupter, Smiler, Shouter in the Night.

Bacchus and Pentheus

TED HUGHES

So the fame of the blind
Seer Tiresias
Blazed up in all the Greek cities.
Only Pentheus, King of Thebes,
Laughed at the old man's prophecies.
'In-fill for empty skulls,'
He jeered at this dreamer.
'Dreams,' he explained,
'Which this methane-mouth
Tells us are the dark manifesto
Of the corrector, are nothing of the kind.
They are corpse-lights, the ignes fatui
Miasma from the long-drop
And fermenting pit
Of what we don't want, don't need,
And have dumped.
They rise from the lower bowel. And lower.'
The laughter of Pentheus
Clanged through his malodorous prisons and echoed
Into the underworld and into heaven.

Tiresias replied with his usual riddle:
'How lucky for you, Pentheus,
If only you, like me, had managed
To get rid of your two eyes
That so sharply
Supervise everything and see nothing.
Then you would not have to watch
What Bacchus will do to you.
These dreams, that you call ridiculous,
And that attract your derision,
Just as your own dear body

Will look like what it is not
Because of a glittering blanket of blowflies—
These dreams
Have shown me this new god, son of Semele,
And they have shown me a preview, in full colour,
Of a banquet
Bacchus will hold for you, Pentheus,
At which you will be not only guest of honour
But the food and the drink. Think of it.
Your expensive coiffure
With your face wrapped in it
Wrenched off like a cork, at the neck,
Your blood
Poured out over your mother and sisters,
Your pedigree carcass
Ripped by unthinking fingers
Into portions, and your blue entrails,
Tangled in thorns and draped over dusty rocks,
Tugged at by foxes.
All this, Pentheus, as clear as if
It had already happened. I saw it
In a silly dream
Which this new god, outlawed by you,
Gave to me on a street corner.
Gave to me—for me to give to you.
What can it mean?'

Pentheus with a roar
Kicked the old blind man
Like a stray befouling dog
From his palace. A lifetime too late
To alter himself or his fate.

The god has come. The claustrophobic landscape
Bumps like a drum
With the stamping dance of the revellers.
The city pours

Its entire population into the frenzy.
Children and their teachers, labourers, bankers,
Mothers and grandmothers, merchants, agents,
Prostitutes, politicians, police,
Scavengers and accountants, lawyers and burglars,
Builders, layabouts, tradesmen, con men,
Scoundrels, tax collectors, academicians,
Physicians, morticians, musicians, magicians,
The idle rich and the laughing mob
Stretched mouths in glazed faces,
All as if naked anonymous freed
Into the ecstasy
The dementia and the delirium
Of the new god.

Pentheus rushes about, his voice cracks.
He screams like an elephant:
'This is a disease—
Toads have got into the wells,
The granaries have all gone to fungus,
A new flea is injecting bufotenin.
You forget, you Thebans,
You are the seed of the god Mars.
Remember your ancestry
Under the tongue of the great serpent
Inaccessible to folly.
You veterans, what has happened to your hearing—
It was cured and seasoned
By the crash of weaponry and the war-cries
And the dying cries of the enemy.
How can you go capering
After a monkey stuffed with mushrooms?
How can you let yourselves be bitten
By this hopping tarantula
And by these glass-eyed slavering hydrophobes?
You pioneers, you first settlers, heroes,
You who raised our city, stone by stone,
Out of the slime of the salt marsh,

And hacked its roof-tree, with your sword's edge,
Out of the very solar system
To shield a night light for your babes and toddlers,
How can you
Go rolling your eyes and waggling your fingers
After that claque of poltroons?
Remember
How often you dragged yourselves, by your teeth and nails,
Out of the mass graves
And the fields of massacre,
Clutching your wives and new-born,
Fighting off the hyenas—
Can a fed-back, millionfold
Amplified heartbeat
And some drunken woman's naked heel tossed over your heads
Bounce you out of your wits—
Like bobbing unborn babies?
Iron warriors, menhirs of ancient manhood,
Tootling flutes
Wet as spaghetti?
And you philosophers,
Metaphysicians, where are your systems?
What happened to the great god Reason?
And to the stone table of Law
That you fitted back together
Out of the Absolute's shattering anger
Against backsliders—
You have become sots,
You have dunked it all, like a donut,
Into a mugful of junk music—
Which is actually the belly-laugh
Of this androgynous, half-titted witch.
You are forgetting the other.
You forget the hard face of the future
With its hungry mouth and its cry
Which is the battle-cry
That waits behind the time of plenty
Greedy for all you have,

And that massacres for amusement, for thrills,
And will liberate your homes and your land
From your possession.
You forget the strangers who are not friendly.
They are coming over the earth's bulge
Out of the wombs of different mothers,
As sure as the moon's tide,
To lift off your roofs and remove your walls like driftwood
And take all you have.
With ground steel they will separate you from it
Leaving you hugging the burnt earth.
If Thebes has to fall
That would be better.
We could succumb to such a fate with honour.
Then our despair would resemble a noble trophy,
Our tears would be monumental.
But you have surrendered the city
Not to war's elemental chaos
And heroes harder and readier than yourselves
But to a painted boy, a butterfly face,
Swathed in glitter.
A baboon
Got up as an ear-ring
In the ear of a jigging whore.

'As for this lewd, blasphemous joke
About his birth—
Begotten by God himself, a divine by-blow,
Then snatched by his father's scorched fingers
Out of the incineration of his mother—
Sodden, squirming, no bigger than a newt,
Then gestated full term, an implant,
In the thigh of Almighty God.
By which he implies—like a papoose
In God's scrotum.
Do you hear this fairy tale?
How can you swallow it? Bring the juggler to me.
Let me get my thumbs on that Adam's apple,

I'll pop this lie out of him, with squeals,
Like the pip of yellow
Out of a boil. Like a pulp of maggot,
A warble-fly chrysalis
From under the hide of a bull.
Bring him.'

With the dry foam framing his lips
Pentheus sent his praetorian guard
To arrest this creature, this Bacchus,
Acclaimed as a new god.

His grandfather, blear-eyed but long-sighted,
Tried to restrain him.
The wise elders, too tottery and arthritic
To go dancing, tried to restrain him.
Their warnings fell like holy water sprinkled
Onto a pan of boiling pig-fat.
Their head-shakings, white-haired, white bearded,
Like a log-jam in a big river
Only broke his momentum into bellowings,
Frothings, and the plunge
Of a cataract.

The guards come back bruised and dishevelled.
They bring to Pentheus not the Bacchus he wanted
But a different prisoner. They call him
'A priest of the new rites.'
Hands bound, a jackal-faced Etruscan.
Pentheus' glare, a white-hot branding-iron,
Bears down on the face of this prisoner.
With difficulty he calms
His homicidal hands, as he speaks.
'Your death approaches
Very fast, simply because
Your friends need the warning. So: quickly:
What is your homeland, your family and your name.
And how does it come about

That you end up here, the manikin doll
Of this ventriloqual, mesmeric,
Itinerant common fraud?'

The voice that answers him is quite fearless.
'I am Acoetes, out of Maeonia.
My parents were poor.
My father possessed neither stock
Nor ground for it to stand on.
His wealth
Was a barbed hook and the art
Of finding fish with it.
These, and the wilderness of waters,
Were his bequest to me.
But I grew weary of wading among herons.
I took to open water.
I pushed a prow out through breakers.
I stretched my cunning
Between the tiller, the sail
And the constellations.
As I learned the moods
Of the menagerie of heaven—
Of squally Capricornus, the saturnine goat,
Of the Hyades, the little piglets
Showering summer stars,
Of the two bears revolving in their clock,
All the winds of ocean
Became familiar, and their safe havens.

'One time,
My destination Delos, I was blown
Onto the coast of Chios.
Skill with the oars got us ashore safely.
That night we camped there. At dawn
I sent Opheltes, the bosun, with men
To find fresh water,
While I climbed a headland
To study the wind, the sky-signs, the horizons.

Everything looked promising. I returned
To the ship, recalling my crew.
"Look what we've found," shouted Opheltes.
He shoved ahead of him a strange boy,
A little boy, beautiful as a girl.
They'd picked him up on the hillside.
Straight away they'd recognized plunder.
The child staggered,
Mouth half open, eyelids heavy.
He was ready to collapse
With wine, or sleep, or both.
But I saw, I knew, by everything
About him, this boy was more than mortal.
His face, his every movement,
Told me he was a god.
I said to the crew: "I do not know
Which god you have found but I am certain
This child is divine."
Then I spoke to the boy: "Whoever you are
Preserve our lives in the sea, bless our voyage,
And forgive these fellows
Their rough words and their rough hands."

' "None of that rubbish," cried Dictys. "This boy's ours."
His anger was quick—like his body,
Quickest of all, like a gibbon
To hurtle here and there in the ship's rigging.
Libys roared agreement. He was a dullard.
Always feeling he was being robbed
Or outwitted, always wanting a fight.
Melanthus joined them—he was sharper, our look-out,
But bored with too much emptiness
On both sides of his blond eyelashes.
Alcemidon likewise. He thought only
Of what he could get away with.
And black Epopeus, whose voice was a maul,
Literally, one huge muscle
All to itself, the timekeeper

And metronome of the oarsmen,
Always craving for exercise. And the rest
They bent their voices to his
Just as out on the sea they bent their bodies.
The girlish boy
Was a landfall, a whole port
For these testy sailors. But I blocked
The top of the gangplank.
"Bestial sacrilege," I told them,
"Shall not defile this vessel
While I am master of it."

'The worst man among them pretended to retch.
Lycabas. He was so reckless
He seemed to be searching everywhere
With a kind of desperation
For his own violent death.
Tuscany had thrown him out
For murdering a neighbour.
He grabbed at my throat with his rower's fingers
And would have pitched me overboard
But I caught hold of a rope, and between my knee
And his pelvic bone
Gave his testicles the fright of their lives.
The whole crew bellowed, with one voice,
For him to get up
And finish what he had started.
The uproar
Seemed to rouse the boy.
The great god Bacchus awoke.
"My friends," he cried,
"What was that awful noise? It sounded awful!
Where am I? How did I get here?
Are you planning to take me somewhere?
Tell me where."'
Proreus found a soft voice.
"Nothing to be afraid of. You seemed lost.
We thought you'd like a lift.

Where do you want to go?
Wherever you say—and we'll drop you off."
Then the god said:
"Naxos is my home. Take me there
And many friends for life
Will give you a welcome to remember."

'Those criminals
With sudden hilarity
Swore by the sea and all its gods to take him.
And they urged me to get under way—
To do the boy this easy favour.
I took them at their word
Since Lycabas still sprawled
Groaning and vomiting in the scuppers.
I set the painted prow
Towards Naxos.

'Then Opheltes, in a hissing whisper,
Asked me if I was crazy.
And the rest of the crew, their faces,
Their mouthings, their gestures, made it plain—
They wanted me to take the boy where they pleased
Very far from Naxos.

'I could not believe
They could suppose a god could be tricked by men.
I told them:
"This is not only wrong—it is foolhardy.
I'll have no part in it."
Then one of them, Aethalion,
Shouldered me from the helm.
"In that case," he said, "leave our fortunes to us."

'As the ship heeled, the god of actors
Went reeling off balance. He clutched the gunwale,
Stared at the churned swerve in the wake
And pretended to weep.

"This is not the way home," he wailed.
"The sun should be on that side. We were
Right before. What have I done wrong?
What is the world going to say
If the whole crew of you
Kidnap one small boy?"
Those bandits laughed at his tears
And they laughed at me, too, for mine.
But I swear
By the god himself
(And there is no god closer, to hear me)
That the incredible
Truly now did happen.

'First, the ship stops dead in the sea
As if rammed into a dry dock.
The oarsmen are amazed. They grimace
And force the blood from under their fingernails
To budge the hull or shear the rowlocks.
The sails are helpless,
Flogging in their ropes. Then suddenly ivy
Comes swarming up the oars, it cumbers the oar-strokes
And tumbles in over the deck,
Coiling up the masts, boiling over
To spill great bundles, swinging in the wind,
Draping the sails. And the god
Is standing there, mid-ship, crowned
With clusters of fat grapes.
He brandishes a javelin
Twined with stems and leaves of the vine.
And around him are heaped, as if real,
The great shapes of big cats, yawning, blinking,
The striped and the spotted, leopards, lynxes,
Tigers and jungle cats.

'Then either in panic terror or godsent madness
Every man leaps up, as if for his life,
And overboard into the sea.

Medon was the first to go black.
His spine arched into a half-wheel, mid-air.
Lycabas gibbered at him. "Look, he's changing
Into a sea-monster—"
As his own gape widened
Backward beneath his ears, his nose flattened,
His body slicked smooth, his skin toughened.
And Libys—his hands slipped from the oar
Because they were already shrinking.
Before he hit the wave he knew they were fins.
Another was reaching up
To free the ropes from the ivy
And found he had no arms. With a howl
He somersaulted over the stern
In a high arc
Flailing the black half-moon of a tail
That had replaced his legs.
These creatures crash round the ship.
They fling sheets of spray over the ivy
As they plunge under. Or they burst upwards
Like a troupe of acrobatic dancers—
Blasting out in a fume, through their blowholes,
The sea they gulp as they frolic.
I was the survivor of twenty,
Shuddering with fear, barely sane.
But the god was kind.
"Now steer towards Dia," he told me.
And I did so. And there I was rewarded.
I entered the priesthood of this mighty god.'

Then Pentheus spoke:
'You have dreamed us a long dream,
With a deal of ocean bluster,
But my anger has neither slept nor cooled.'
He called for slaves.
'Break this man on the rack elaborately.
Send him down to hell grateful
For the respite.'

So Acoetes was dragged off, and slammed
Into a strongroom.
But it is told:
While the executioner's implements
Of fire, pincers, choppers and incidentals,
Were being readied
To gratify Pentheus, of a sudden
Bolts shot out of their sockets and went skittering
Over the floors. Locks exploded
In a scatter of components curiously fractured.
Doors flew open untouched.
And untouched the shackles
Fell off Acoetes.

Pentheus heard of this. But from it
Learned nothing. Instead, his brain temperature
Rose a degree. Something insane
Behind his eyes
Tore off its straitjacket.
He thought no more of bodyguards
Than of jailors, warders, doctors, nurses.
Alone he climbed Cithaeron,
The mountain consecrated to Bacchus,
Where the air
Pounded his eardrums like mad fists
And seemed to pound in his heart,
And the screaming songs of the possessed
Were like the screams of a horse, resounding
Inside the horse's own skull.
Pentheus was like that horse
On a battlefield, when the unfought fury
Shimmers in mid-air before the attack,
And the blast of the trumpets
Goes like lightning
Through every supercharged nerve,
And he whinnies, rolls his eyeballs,
Champs foam and paws at the far sky
To be first at the enemy—

Pentheus was like that
When he heard the unbearable howls
And ululations
Of the Bacchantes, and the clash of their cymbals.
And when he tripped in his fury
And fell on all fours,
When he clutched the sod and felt their stamping
Shaking the mountain under his fingers,
When Pentheus
Saw the frightened worms
Twisting up out of their burrows
Then the red veil came over his vision.

Halfway up the slope is a level clearing.
Pentheus bounded into it and halted—
Too astonished to take cover,
Utterly unprepared
For what he had surprised.
He stared, in a stupor,
Into the naked mysteries.

The first to see him,
The first to come for him
Like a bear defending her cubs,
The first to drive her javelin into him
Was his own mother—
Screeching as she came:
'It's the boar that ploughed up our gardens!
I've hit it! Quickly, sisters, now we can kill it!
I've hit it!' Pentheus falls
And the whole horde of women
Pile on top of him
Like a pack of wild dogs,
Like a squabbling heap of vultures
Every one tries to get hold of something
And pull it away.

A changed man, Pentheus,
Emptied with terror,
Tries to crawl.
His mouth bites at new words,
Strange words, words that curse himself,
That renounce himself, that curse Pentheus.
He convicts himself,
Begs for forgiveness
With blood coming out of his mouth.
He heaves upright,
Shouting to his aunt: 'Autone,
Remember your darling Actaeon
Torn to rags by the hounds that loved him.
Pity me.' The name Actaeon
Sounds to her like the scream of a pig
As she wrenches his right arm
Out of its socket and clean off.
While Ino, with the strength of the god,
Twists and tears off the other.
Armless, he lurches towards his mother.
'Mother,' he sobs, 'Mother, look at me,
Recognize me, Mother!'
Agave stares, she blinks, her mouth wide.
She takes her son's head between her hands,
Gazes a moment,
Then rips it from his shoulders.
She lifts it, like a new-born baby,
Her red fingers hooked into the hair
Letting the blood splash over her face and breasts—
'Victory!' she shrieks. 'I've done it! I did it!'

Swiftly, like a light breeze at dawn,
After the first hard night-frost
Has left a tree's leaves
Precariously attached,
So swiftly

The hands of those women
Separated the king's bones and stripped them.

The lesson
Was not lost on Thebes, the city of letters.
Women made sure, thereafter,
That this sleepy child
Was acknowledged, was honoured
And made happy by all who played with him
In his ritual play,
Blessing all who blessed him.

Pyramus and Thisbe

FRED D'AGUIAR

Pyramus to Thisbe

The wall between our love
Stands as neat as foxgloves.
We whisper through a chink.
Our mixed breaths is our link
Doing what two lovers might
If the climate was right.

Deep and wide as an ocean
Between me and my woman,
Semiramis's wall is cold,
Dark, rough and solid:
Anti-love, anti-loving,
Anti-life, anti-everything.

But our breaths mix halfway
In that wall and must play
Out what two lovers would
Just do, if only they could
Meet and touch as we can't,
Haven't, mustn't, badly want.

We've met and done, my love,
All that lovers think of,
Except all's in our head
And heart, so, good as dead.
When I press against her,
She matches my pressure

Exactly, always; that thing
put there by those who think

love between us is a joke.
Let's show them in one stroke.
Elope with me, my baby;
Be my midnight lady.

I am black and you're white:
What's the day without night
To measure it by and give
It definition; life.
We'll go where love's colour-
Blind and therefore coloured.

Join me under the tree
At Ninus's tomb at 3
a.m., everyone's asleep
Then, you won't hear a peep
Out of them. They will wake
Missing us far too late.

Us two, safe in some land
Where people understand
Love, whatever colour, shape
Or size it may appear;
Where they don't sling insults
Forcing our love to skulk

Underground, or as we're
Reduced to, run from here.
Meet me by that mulberry,
Eat its sheer-white cherries,
Sample the nearby spring,
If you can beat my sprint

Or by a secret route
Reach there first, which I doubt.
I don't question your speed
(Since our love's fleetfooted).

Not seeing you, I speak
Unsurely, sound upbeat.

Thisbe to Pyramus

This mulberry tree
Leaning at the spring
Where you said, meet me?
Its fruit tastes of sin.

I stood there trembling
An eternity,
Or what resembled
An eternity.

Tree, fruit and cool spring,
That entire place,
Paled, paled to nothing,
Then just the big face

Fronting that lion
Bloody from a kill,
And smelling human
Flesh, made wilder still.

Pyramus, I swear
I ran faster than
You, into a cave.
It fell from my hand . . .

I would have turned back
For that crucial shawl
Risking my own neck,
Than you find it mauled

And, thinking me dead
From all that fresh blood

And fabric in shreds,
Run, run yourself through!

Death's the wall between
Us now; the wall seen
From life, none can see
Unless death agrees.

How fast you scaled that!
Who's to win this race?
You, for your swift death
Sure I was savaged?

Or me seeing this:
You, all warm, bloody,
And knowing the gist
Of it's you loved me?

Your wet blade's sweet tip
Is hardly in me;
Already the fruit
Turn red on the tree.

Salmacis and Hermaphroditus

TED HUGHES

Among those demi-gods, those perfect girls
Who sport about the bright source and live in it,
The beauty of Salmacis, the water-nymph,
Was perfect,
As among damselflies a damselfly's,
As among vipers the elegance
Of a viper, or a swan's grace among swans.
She was bending to gather lilies for a garland
When she spied Hermaphroditus.
At that first glimpse she knew she had to have him.
She felt she trod on prickles until she could touch him.
She held back only a moment,
Checked her girdle, the swing of her hem, her cleavage,
Let her lust flood hot and startled
Into her cheek, eyes, lips—made her whole face
Open as a flower that offers itself,
Wet with nectar, then she spoke:
'Do you mind if I say—you are beautiful?
Seen from where I stand, you could be a god.
Are you a god? If you are human
What a lucky sister! As for the mother
Who held you, and pushed her nipple between your lips,
I am already sick with envy of her.
I dare not think of a naked wife in your bed.
If she exists, I dare not think of her bliss.
Let me beg a taste, one little sip
Of her huge happiness. A secret between us.
But if you are unmarried—here I am.
Let us lie down and make our own
Bridal bed, where we can love each other
To sleep. And awaken each other.'

The boy blushed—he had no idea
What she was talking about.
Her heart lurched again when she saw
How his blush bewildered his beauty,
Like the red side of an apple against a sunset,
Or the ominous dusky flush
That goes over the cold moon
When the eclipse grips its edge
And begins to swallow it inch by inch
In spite of all the drums and pans and gongs
Beaten on earth beneath to protect it.

Then the nymph slid her arms
Around his neck, and asked for a kiss,
One kiss, one brotherly kiss—
'Get away,' he cried. 'Let me go,
Or I'm off. And you can sit here
On your basket of tricks all by yourself!'
That scared Salmacis, she thought he really might go.
'Oh no, forgive me!' she sobbed. 'Forgive me!
I couldn't help it. I'm going. Oh, I'm spoiling
This lovely place for you. I'm going. I'm going.'

So, lingering her glances, she goes.
And truly she seems to have gone.
In fact, she has ducked behind a bush.
There she kneels, motionless, head lifted—
Her eye fixed, like the eye of a leopard.
He plays, careless as a child,
Roams about happily
Thinking he's utterly alone.
He paddles into the pool's edge, goes deeper.
The cool pulse of the spring, warping the clarity,
Massages his knees, delicious.
He peels off his tunic and the air
Makes free with all that had been hidden,
Freshens his nudity. Under the leaves

Salmacis groaned softly
And began to tremble.
As the sun
Catches a twisting mirror surface
With a splinter of glare
Her own gaze flamed and hurt her. She was already
Up and leaping towards him,
She had grabbed him with all her strength—
Yet still she crouched where she was
Shaking all over, letting this go through her
Like a dreadful cramp. She watched him
Slap his pale shoulders, hugging himself,
And slap his belly to prepare it
For the plunge—then plunge forward.
And suddenly he was swimming, a head bobbing,
Chin surging through the build of a bow-wave,
Shoulders liquefied,
Legs as if at home in the frog's grotto,
Within a heave of lustre limpid as air
Like a man of ivory glossed in glass,
Or a lily in a bulb of crystal.

'I've won!' shrieked Salmacis. 'He's mine!'
She could not help herself.
'He's mine!' she laughed to nobody in particular
And with a couple of bounds
Hit the pool stark naked
In a rocking crash and thump of water—
The slips of her raiment settling wherever
They happened to fall. Then out of the upheaval
Her arms grab and wind round him,
And slippery as the roots of big lilies
But far stronger, her legs wind round him.
He flounders and goes under. All his strength
Fighting to get back up through a cloud of bubbles
Leaves him helpless to her burrowing kisses.
Burning for air, he can do nothing
As her hands hunt over him, and as her body

Knots itself every way around him
Like a sinewy otter
Hunting some kind of fish
That flees hither and thither inside him;
And as she flings and locks her coils
Around him like a snake
Around the neck and legs and wings of an eagle
That is trying to fly off with it;
And like ivy which first binds the branches
In its meshes, then pulls the whole tree down;
And as the octopus—
A tangle of constrictors, nippled with suckers,
That drag towards a maw—
Embraces its prey.

But still Hermaphroditus kicks to be free
And will not surrender
Or yield her the least kindness
Of the pleasure she longs for,
And rages for, and pleads for
As she crushes her breasts and face against him
And clings to him as with every inch of her surface.
'It's no good struggling,' she hisses.
'You can strain, wrestle, squirm, but cannot
Ever get away from me now.
The gods are listening to me.
The gods have agreed we never never
Shall be separated, you and me.'
The gods heard her frenzy—and smiled.
And there in the dizzy boil the two bodies
Melted into a single body
Seamless as the water.

Cadmus

CRAIG RAINE

the skin on his forearms
like the skin on egg custard

his past   coming and going
a dream in the daze of dying

he is in the Post Office
drinking tea   his children
were drowned   were changed
into gods
a moth was magnetized
to the glass
Halloween pumpkin eyes
elephants slobbering

you have to drink tea
and eat and go to the toilet
carefully   you have to concentrate
you can fall anywhere

in the Post Office

a pupa
of chewing gum under the counter

when his skin begins to change
he begins to leave it behind
pulling his body over his body
over his head

dark   tight tight

he shrugs his shoulders off
the ears are difficult

unrecognizable
his aura of cling film
stuck to the carpet tiles

he feels

slim   tight as a woven whip
quilted   bead embroidery
new Missoni knitwear
beautiful again

upper set broken in two
his unintelligible lisp

when they bring a mirror
to test for breath
he sees a snake

wait
no
mistake
mistake

Atlas

MICHAEL HOFMANN

He went West, drifted
through the Italo-Western desert,
bluffs, razor-wire, Coppertone,
to the paranoid steers' heads
of Atlas' spread.
He nosed along the wire,
grazing beasts in their thousands,
through to the sea.
A peon took him to Atlas.
They spoke under a greenback tree,
the bark was singles, the leaves tens,
the fruit hundreds. He didn't know
where to look, the man-mountain
or his millions. He blurted out
his request, something to eat
and a place to stay. 'I'm the son
of God. If you treat me real nice
he'll pay you out.
I may be just a kid,
but I been in with some fellows
I can tell you about.' Atlas
had been tipped off. Verbum sap.
A guy shooting this kind of line
about gods and great deeds
was coming to get his tree.
'Son, if your daddy's not
who you say he is, and your deeds
are nothing special, you in big trouble.
Now get out of here, before
I make you.' Perseus talked back,
pleaded with him, got fresh.
He grabbed him by the scruff,

lifted him clean off the ground,
carried him straight-armed
off his property like a kicking
jackrabbit and dropped him.
Red with shame and exertion,
Perseus went for his big shooter,
a museum piece, his grandmother's.
He looked the other way,
and let him have it, both barrels.
Atlas stiffened and went all big on him,
went slope, scree, treeline,
col, ridge, dome, peak.
It was really neat.

Perseus and Andromeda

PETER READING

Aeolus stilled the winds, and the dawn star
    rose up refulgent
ushering mortals to get to their business.
    Perseus, rising,
put on his swift-winged sandals and with his
    hooked sword ascended,
cleaving the clear air, leaving behind him
    numerous nations,
coming at last to Cepheus' kingdom.
    Here was Andromeda,
unjustly fettered to pay for the heinous
    crime of her mother
(Cassiopeia—Cepheus' wife—had
    angered Neptune,
boasting herself more beautiful than his
    Nereid maidens).

Perseus saw her, chain-bound there to the
    sea-battered cliff-face,
would have assumed her an alabaster
    monument, but that
hair from her forehead stirred in the wind and
    tears from her eyes welled.
Then he fell deeply besotted in love with her,
    stunned by her beauty—
almost forgetting to ply his heels' pinions,
    such was his wonder.
Landing, he cried: 'You shouldn't be bound in
    chains made of metal;
rather, the links that bond lovers should be
    yours.' And he asked her
what was her name and her nation, and the

reason she suffered.
Being a virgin, she wouldn't presume to
      speak to a stranger,
modestly would have hidden her face in her
      hands, had they been free.
Freely, however, her eyes shed tears as
      Perseus persisted.
Then, lest her silence might seem to imply some
      culpable conduct,
hapless Andromeda told him her name and
      that of her nation,
how she was fettered unjustly for the
      crime of her mother,
there to endure an ocean monster's
      molestations.

While she was speaking the waters roared and,
      breasting the broad waves,
out of the dolorous deep advanced a
      menacing ogre.
Shrilly she screamed. Her father and mother
      (more so the latter)
each felt an impotent wretchedness, only
      able to wail grief,
clinging the while to the chained girl, making
      loud lamentations.
Perseus then addressed them: 'The time for
      grief is unending;
time for actively helping, however, is
      dreadfully short-lived.
If I were now to tell you that I am
      Perseus, son of
Danaë and Jupiter, Perseus who slew the
      serpent-haired Gorgon,
Perseus who dared to brave the winds on
      feathery pinions,
then I should prove myself eligible to
      marry your daughter.

If I now add to these credentials
    that of my service
(should the gods favour me), surely you'll have to
    give me your blessing.'
This they agreed (in addition, a dowry)—
    who could refuse it?

Then, as the beak of a galley, driven
    hard by her rowers,
furrows the foam, so the monster's sternum
    parted the water.
Now it was only a stone's throw from where they
    stood at the cliff-base.
Suddenly Perseus sprung from the earth, rose
    up to the high clouds.
Seeing his shadow traversing the sea, the
    monster attacked it.
Just as an eagle, sighting a basking
    snake in a sunned field,
stoops on the scaled neck, deeply embedding
    dagger-sharp talons
lest the infuriated reptile
    twists its fangs backwards,
so, swooping swiftly, Perseus burst through the
    air in a steep dive,
buried his sword to the hilt in the monster's
    bellowing body.
Goaded, enraged by the wound, the brute thrashed
    rearing and plunging,
spinning around like the fierce wild boar when
    baying hounds bait it.
Deftly avoiding the greedily snapping
    maw of the monster,
plying his pinions, the hero struck its
    barnacled hump-back,
thrusting his curved blade deep in its ribs and
    slashing the finned tail.
Spray from the gushes of purple vomit

spewed by the monster
    spattered the wings of Perseus, made them
        heavy with blood spume.
Fearing to trust these gore-drenched pinions
        further, the hero
reached for a rock projecting above the
        wind-lashed surface.
Bracing himself, he firmly gripped this
        crag with his left hand,
thrusting his blade with his right hand repeatedly
        into the beast's guts—
Olympus itself, as well as the common
        people, applauded.

Cassiopeia and Cepheus, joyous,
        lauded the hero,
calling him son-in-law, saying he'd saved their
        house from destruction.
Unchained, the reason/reward for this feat of
        daring descended;
meanwhile the victor cleansed his hands in the
        brine which they brought him.
So that Medusa's snake-haired head might
        suffer no damage,
thickly he laid down leaves on the ground and
        over them seaweed,
placing the head of the Gorgon on top of them.
        Living, absorbent,
freshly gathered, the seaweed fronds turned
        stony and brittle—
just as today all corals retain this
        quality, pliant
under the water but petrifying when
        brought to the surface.

Perseus then built altars of turf to
        honour three godheads:
one to Minerva, on which a cow was

  sacrificed duly;
next he dispatched a calf in homage to
  wing-footed Mercury;
finally, slaying a bull, he elicited
  Jupiter's favour.
Claiming Andromeda now as his prize for so
  worthy an exploit,
Perseus sought no more dowry, but straightway
  moved to the feast where
Cupid and Hymen presided fuelling
  fires with rich incense.
Garlands festooned the roof-tree; joyful
  harps and flutes sounded;
huge folding doors flung back to reveal a great
  golden interior;
sumptuous then was the banquet laid for
  Cepheus' courtiers.

When it was finished and all had indulged in
  bacchic cavortings,
Perseus asked his hosts about local
  customs and manners.
One of them answered him, adding: 'Now tell us,
  valiant Perseus,
how you beheaded the Gorgon Medusa.' The
  hero explained how
under cold Atlas there was a place whose
  entrance was guarded
closely by two hag sisters who shared one
  eyeball between them;
while it was being transferred from one to the
  other, he stole it,
then travelled far through trackless rock-strewn
  forests, arriving
finally where the Gorgons dwelt—on
  all sides around him,

petrified beasts and men, all changed by
　　glimpsing Medusa.
He hadn't looked direct in her face but had
　　rather observed her
safely by way of the image reflected
　　bright in his bronze shield.
She and her snakes were asleep when he severed her
　　head from her shoulders;
fleet-winged Pegasus and his brother were
　　born from her spilt blood.

Further, the hero told of more dangers
　　bravely encountered:
oceans and lands he had witnessed, even
　　stars he had soared to,
bold on his beating wings. When he had finished,
　　still they were eager—
one of his hearers asked why, of all the
　　Gorgon sisters,
only Medusa had tresses of coiling
　　hideous serpents.
'Since what you ask is of interest to all men,
　　I will inform you.
She was once famed for her loveliness, sought by
　　passionate suitors,
fairest of all of her attributes was her
　　hair (I was told this
thing by a man I once met who claimed to have
　　seen her in those days).
Neptune, however, ravished the maid in
　　Minerva's temple,
whereupon modest Minerva hid her
　　face with her aegis,
punished the Gorgon by changing her locks to these
　　writhing reptiles.
Now, on her corselet, Minerva still wears the
　　likeness of serpents;

still, on the goddess's breastplate are etched these
    terrible emblems.'

•

[Perseus, freeing Andromeda from her
    fetters, restored her
safe to the arms of her overjoyed father, who
    offered the hero
any reward he desired—and was answered: 'The
    hand of your daughter.'
Cepheus consented (albeit she was al-
    ready betrothed to
Phineus, her uncle). The marriage feast was
    duly appointed . . .]

To the assembled guests in the royal
    court of King Cepheus,
valiant Perseus was retailing deeds of
    personal prowess.
Suddenly, raucous howls of a riot
    rived the serene hall
(clearly no hymn to Hymen, but some
    presage of mayhem),
as a calm sea is whipped by a squall to
    furious breakers.

Phineus irrupted, leading the mob with a
    bronze-pointed ash spear
(out to avenge what he saw as the theft of his
    promised Andromeda),
aimed it at Perseus, tensed for the throw, but
    Cepheus held him:
'Brother, what madness impels you to this grave
    criminal action?
It wasn't Perseus who stole your bride, but
    malicious Neptune.
Perseus saved her from being molested;
    you lacked the courage;

let him who rescued her marry her, for my
    word has been given.'

Phineus glowered at his brother and then at his
    rival, uncertain
which to attack. Then a violent spasm
    gripped the aggressor;
harmless, his flung spear splintered the bench where
    Perseus was seated.
Up leaped the hero, tugged the wedged weapon
    loose and relaunched it.
Phineus dodged it, diving behind the
    altar for cover.
Rhoetus, however, stood in the path of the
    terrible javelin,
full in the face he was struck by the bronze spike,
    sunk to the floor, felled;
when the cold metal was wrenched from his cloven
    face-bones his heels drummed,
kicking convulsively, then the spread tables were
    spattered with blood gouts.

Baying for spilt guts, the rest of the rabble
    took up their weapons,
Some of them yowling that Cepheus ought to
    perish with Phineus—
Cepheus, however, had already left the
    palace, invoking
Justice and Faith and the Gods of Hospi-
    tality, saying
how he abhorred this outrage. Meanwhile,
    bellicose Pallas
flew to the aid of Perseus with the
    strength of her aegis.

There was an Indian, Athis, a handsome
    youth of just sixteen,
rich robes enhancing his beauty, a gold chain

gracing his neck, his
     ringlets, adorned with a golden headband,
          perfumed with sweet myrrh—
Athis, renowned for hurling the javelin,
          famed as an archer.
Now the boy bent his bow, Perseus seized a
          brand from the altar,
swung the still-smouldering cudgel, smashed it
          into the lovely
features; the face was instantly splattered,
          pulped into flenched mash.
Athis' lover, Lycabas, when he
          saw the boy dying,
wept for the mangled youthfulness, paused and
          snatched up the strung bow:
'Now you have me to contend with, not for
          long will you triumph
over the death of a boy whose slaying
          does you no credit—
merely arouses contempt.' And the arrow
          sped from the bowstring.
Missing its target, it lodged in the sleeve of
          Perseus' garment.
Then the great hero wielded his falchion
          (that which had severed
Gorgon Medusa's hideous head) and
          lunged into Lycabas.
Lycabas, moribund, crawled to the place where
          Athis' body
lay, and he fell there, soon to expire with
          this consolation:
even in death there is comfort through sharing,
          joined with a loved friend.

Two more, Phorbas and Amphimedon, were
          eager to join in,
slipped on the blood that flooded the floor and
          slid in the offal.

As they attempted to regain their balance
    Perseus was at them,
thrust his curved blade through the ribcage of one and the
    throat of the other.

Eurytus came next, wielding a lethal
    two-bladed battleaxe.
Perseus dispatched him by lifting a massive
    amphora (ornate,
richly embossed) and crashing it heavily
    on his opponent—
Eurytus spewed blood, fell on his back and,
    agonized, twitching,
beat his smashed head on the smirched floor. Then in
    rapid succession
Perseus slaughtered royal Polydaemon,
    Abaris, Clytus,
Lycetus, Phlegyas, Helices . . . all the while
    trampling corpses.

Phineus didn't dare tackle his foe in
    hand-to-hand combat.
Hurling his spear, he missed and struck Idas
    (who, until now, had
sided with nobody). Idas tugged out the
    javelin, snarling:
'Phineus, you force me to face you in conflict;
    you shall pay dearly.'
He was about to heave back the weapon when
    loss of blood felled him.

Hodites then was carved up by Clymenus,
    Hypseus struck down
Prothoenor, and Hypseus in turn was
    butchered by Perseus . . .

There was an old man, Emathion, who was
    just and god-fearing—

age kept him out of the fray, but his sharp tongue
        served as a weapon.
Now he stepped forward and called down a curse on
        causeless aggression.
As he was clinging with trembling hands to the
        altar, a sword-stroke
wielded by Chromis sliced off his head, which
        fell on the altar,
there to exhale its last in the altar-fire,
        still execrating.

Then the twin brothers, Broteas and Ammon,
        consummate boxers
(boxing-gloves, though, are no match against cold steel),
        fell to cruel Phineus;
likewise Ampycus, a priest of Ceres.

        Standing aside was
hapless Lampetides, poet/musician,
        there for the wedding,
nervously plucking his harp-strings—the sound was
        heard by Petalus:
'Go sing the rest of your dirge to the ghosts in
        Hades!' he taunted,
driving his sword through the dome of the useless
        poet's left temple.
Groaning and twanging discordantly, he went
        down in a welter.

Irate Lycormas, avenging this outrage,
        ripped out a door-jamb,
smashed it down onto the neck of Petalus (who
        sunk like a slain bull).

One called Pelates was trying to wrench the
        jamb from the other
side, when his palm was pinned to the post by

Corythus' flung spear,
so that he hung by his hand without falling
    when Abas slew him.

Melanus, too, a supporter of Perseus,
    died. Then Dorylas,
one of the wealthiest landowners ever,
    suffered obscenely
when he was speared through the testicles, and his
    callous assailant
commented: 'This, where you lie, is the only
    land you'll be left with.'

Perseus then, to redress this foul slaughter,
    snatched out the shaft (still
warm with the blood of Dorylas) and loosed it
    back at its owner—
in through his nose it thwacked, out through his neckbone.

    Favoured by fortune,
Perseus next slew a couple of brothers,
    Clytius and Clanis
(born of one mother—died of two different wounds):
    Clytius fell when
both of his thighs were skewered by Perseus'
    lethal flung ash-shaft;
Clanis expired with a spear down his throat, teeth
    clenched on the cold spike.

Celadon, Astreus, Aethion (this last
    noted for being
skilled in clairvoyance—albeit he failed to
    forecast his own end),
also Thoactes and infamous parri-
    cidal Agyrtes . . .
all of these fell by the spear or the blade of the
    bloodthirsty hero.

Still there remained more gratuitous violence
        on the agenda.
All the attackers were set to get Perseus,
        ganged up against him,
failed to acknowledge his valour, openly
        countered the king's pledge.
Cepheus' wife and Andromeda filled the
        hall with their shrieking
protests against this atrocity, but their
        outcries were drowned by
clashing of sword-blades and spear-tips and groans of
        agonized dying.
(All the while, blood-loving loathsome Bellona,
        goddess of warfare,
stirred up new trouble, defiling with gore the
        peace of the household.)

Phineus and his thousand supporters
        swarmed about Perseus.
Javelins flew either side of the hero
        thicker than hailstones.
Setting his back to a massive stone column he
        faced the mob's onslaught.
Molpeus led from the left and Ethemon
        rushed on the right flank.
Molpeus he stopped with a slash through the leg, then
        turned his attention
in the direction of frenzied Ethemon, who
        thrust his sword wildly,
hoping to sink it in Perseus' neck but he
        struck the stone column.
Shattered, the steel bounced back at Ethemon and
        stuck in his own throat.
As he stood trembling, suppliant, Perseus
        ran his blade through him.

Finally, Perseus acknowledged that he was
        grossly outnumbered:

'Now you have forced me to summon the help of the
      Gorgon Medusa—
anyone here who is friendly towards me,
      now is the time to
quickly avert your eyes.' Saying which, he raised
      high the appalling
head of the Gorgon. Sceptical Thescalus
      shouldered his javelin:
'Find someone else to intimidate with your
      magical nonsense . . .'
but, as he braced to launch the shaft, he was
      petrified, static.

Ampyx came next, but his sword-thrust at Perseus
      halted in mid-stroke.
Nileus leaped forward proclaiming his greatness,
      threatening Perseus—
suddenly he was cut off in mid-speech, his
      open lips silenced.
Whereupon Eryx upbraided the warriors:
      'It's your own cowardice,
not any mystical power of a hag's head,
      makes you stand rigid!
Rush in with me and we'll overthrow this rash
      youth and his magic!'
As he raced forward he turned to a statue,
      clad in cold granite.

These all deserved the fate meted out by the
      hero; however,
one called Aconteus, Perseus' ally,
      fighting for his cause,
chanced to catch sight of the Gorgon and instantly
      froze into marble.
Thinking him still to be living, Astyagoo
      struck with his long sword
only to hear the steel echoing shrilly
      off the stone statue;

standing amazed, he himself was transformed to
　　stone in a moment.

So many perished that listing them would be
　　too time-consuming.
Only two hundred survivors remained when
　　fighting had finished;
two hundred more glimpsed the head of the Gorgon and
　　turned into cold stone.

Finally, Phineus regretted the conflict
　　which he had started.
Seeing his statuesque forces fixed in
　　various postures,
wildly he called them, touched them, incredulous
　　that they were marble.
Turning away in confession of failure,
　　suppliant Phineus
cried out to Perseus pleadingly, begging:
　　'You are the victor!
Hide it away, that petrifying
　　head of Medusa.
It wasn't hate or ambition that made me
　　bear arms against you.
Why I made war was because of the woman
　　I was betrothed to—
you had done more to deserve her, but I had
　　known her for longer.
I am content to yield, grant me just one thing,
　　greatest of heroes,
only my life.' As he babbled this plea, he
　　didn't dare look up.

'Cowardly Phineus,' Perseus riposted,
　　'do not be fearful.
What I can give you, I will, and don't worry,
　　no sword shall hurt you.
I'll even make you a lasting memorial

here in this palace,
so that my wife may be comforted by the
    sight of her suitor.'

Saying which, Perseus brandished the head of the
    hideous Gorgon
right in the face of the fear-stricken Phineus
    so that he saw it—
tears on his cheeks turned to stone and the craven
    cringing expression,
captured in marble, was permanent, petrified,
    pleading for mercy.

Pyreneus and the Muses

LAWRENCE JOSEPH

But, don't forget, in this, our time,
so much is evil. Do you think a muse

doesn't know evil? One's inspiration
polluted? One's imagination unhinged?

Every day I still see him. The warlord
Pyreneus whose army controlled

the state. We were on Parnassus.
A shadow fell. The dark green air

began to quiver. Huge, widely
spaced drops the heavens exploded.

Two of his boys drove up, told us
to get in out of the rain. Took us

to the villa. Into an inner room.
From his rococo chair upholstered

with silk he arose, arms extended,
to greet us. Designer blue jeans,

T-shirt, yellow linen jacket. Face
puffy and pale. Warm, quiet gaze,

eyes, though, slightly protruding.
A manner which was obsequious

though scary. Whiskey and ice
on the table. He said: I understand

exactly what power is. Understand:
he has deep sympathies, for children

especially. Must force himself
to execute any form of violence.

If only we could see this is his,
his land, by right. He would have been

a connoisseur of art, of music and cinema.
Instead the necessity of history,

obligations of destiny and blood.
Then this: the sky cleared with an eerie

swiftness. Clouds thinned and parted,
a radiant sky. A fresh, electrical

fragrance in the air. We asked to leave.
The doors were locked. We used a window,

flew from there. Pyreneus, then,
as if in a seizure, convinced

he could possess whatever he wanted,
raising himself to his highest power,

waved his arms after us into sky
rushing down like a blazing torrent

around him in darkness, his skull
crashed on the bright green grass.

The Pomegranate

EAVAN BOLAND

puniceum curva decerpserat arbore pomum

The only legend I have ever loved is
The story of a daughter lost in hell.
And found and rescued there.
Love and blackmail are the gist of it.
Ceres and Persephone the names.
And the best thing about the legend is
I can enter it anywhere. And have.
As a child in exile in
A city of fogs and strange consonants,
I read it first and at first I was
An exiled child in the crackling dusk of
The underworld, the stars blighted. Later
I walked out in a summer twilight
Searching for my daughter at bedtime.
When she came running I was ready
To make any bargain to keep her.
I carried her back past whitebeams.
And wasps and honey-scented buddleias.
But I was Ceres then and I knew
Winter was in store for every leaf
On every tree on that road.
Was inescapable for each one we passed.
And for me. It is winter
And the stars are hidden.
I climb the stairs and stand where I can see
My child asleep beside her teen magazines,
Her can of Coke, her plate of uncut fruit.
The pomegranate! How did I forget it?
She could have come home and been safe
And ended the story and all

Our heartbroken searching but she reached
Out a hand and plucked a pomegranate.
She put out her hand and pulled down
The French sound for apple and
The noise of stone and the proof
That even in the place of death,
At the heart of legend, in the midst
Of rocks full of unshed tears
Ready to be diamonds by the time
The story was told, a child can be
Hungry. I could warn her. There is still a chance.
The rain is cold. The road is flint-colored.
The suburb has cars and cable television.
The veiled stars are aboveground.
It is another world. But what else
Can a mother give her daughter but such
Beautiful rifts in time?
If I defer the grief I will diminish the gift.
The legend will be hers as well as mine.
She will enter it. As I have.
She will wake up. She will hold
The papery, flushed skin in her hand.
And to her lips. I will say nothing.

Ascalaphus

CIARAN CARSON

Proserpina ate seven pomegranate seeds. So what? I'll
      tell you what—
It doesn't do to touch strange fruit, when it's forbidden
      by the Powers
That Be. Who put you on a hunger strike, which if you
      break, you'll stay put
In the Underworld. It doesn't do to get caught out.
      Watch out for prowlers.

She'd wandered into Pluto's murky realm; plucked the
      dull-orange bubble.
Split the cortex. Sucked. And who was salivating in the
      bushes' dark interior
But Ascalaphus. Stoolie. Pipsqueak. Mouth. He spilled
      the beans on her, he blabbed—
Straight off he shot, and knocked, knocked, knocked
      on Heaven's iron door.

But she spat back as good as she had got: unholy water
      from the Phlegethon
She slabbered on him. His eyes yellowed, drooled and grew.
      His neb became a beak.
He sprouted spermy wings. Hooked talons shot from his
      fingers. His body dwindled
Into mostly head. All ears, all eyes: touts everywhere,
      potential freaks,

Beware. For now he is the scrake-owl, Troubles' augury
      for Auld Lang Syne,
Who to this day is harbinger of doom, the gloom of
      Pluto's no-go zone.

Arethusa Saved

THOM GUNN

When the god of the river
            pursues her over Greece
weed-rot on his breath
            rape on his mind,
at length Arethusa
            loses her lead,
stops, prays for help
            from a huntress like herself.

Artemis grants her
            ground-fog to hide her
and she cowers wetly
            in condensing cloud
and her own sweat cooling
            from the cross-country run.
Bubbles itch
            in her close-bobbed hair;
where her foot touches
            forms a pool, small
but widening quickly;
            liquid rolls down her,
excessively, really,
            covering her body
till the body is obscured:
            a living sheet of water
has clothed then replaced
            hair, body, and foot.

The river-god roaming
            round the cloud's circumference
sniffing at the edge
            like a dog at a rat-hole

calls out boisterously

     with country-boy bravado

"Arethusa darling

     come out and get screwed."

At last the cloud clears

     —he sees Arethusa

melted to his element,

     a woman of water.

Roaring with joy

     he reverts to river

making to plunge upon her

     and deluge her with dalliance.

But Artemis opened

     many earth-entrances,

cracks underneath her

     hair-thin but deep.

Down them the girl slips

     soaking out of sight

before his glassy stare

     —to be conducted through darkness

to another country,

     Sicily, where she springs

(fountain Arethuse)

     as virgin stream presiding

over pastoral hymn

     with intact hymen,

to be figured on medals

     flanked by fish,

hair caught in a net

     whom the god never netted.

Arachne

THOM GUNN

What is that bundle hanging from the ceiling
Unresting even now with constant slight
Drift in the breeze that breathes through rooms at night?
Can it be something, then, that once had feeling,
A girl, perhaps, whose skill and pride and hope
Strangled against each other in the rope?

I think it is a tangle of despair
As shapeless as a bit of woven nest,
Blackened and matted, quivering without rest
At the mercy of the movements of the air
Where half lodged in, half fallen from the hedge
It hangs tormented at a season's edge.

What an exact artificer she had been!
Her daintiness and firmness are reduced
To lumpy shadow that the dark has noosed.
Something is changing, though. Movements begin
Obscurely as the court of night adjourns,
A tiny busyness at the center turns.

So she spins who was monarch of the loom,
Reduced indeed, but she lets out a fine
And delicate yet tough and tensile line
That catches full day in the little room,
Then sways minutely, suddenly out of sight,
And then again the thread invents the light.

Spiderwoman

MICHAEL LONGLEY

Arachne starts with Ovid and finishes with me.

Her hair falls out and the ears and nostrils disappear
From her contracting face, her body minuscule, thin
Fingers clinging to her sides by way of legs, the rest
All stomach, from which she manufactures gossamer
And so keeps up her former trade, weaver, spider

Enticing the eight eyes of my imagination
To make love on her lethal doily, to dangle sperm
Like teardrops from an eyelash, massage it into her
While I avoid the spinerets—navel, vulva, bum—
And the widening smile behind her embroidery.

She wears our babies like brooches on her abdomen.

Niobe

WILLIAM LOGAN

The upland farmers are a breed apart,
tight with their money, close-mouthed, decent folk
who'd hay your lower pasture twice a year
if you caught sick, but wouldn't give a dime
to charity. They might just burn you out
if you argued with them over politics.
Up there you wouldn't sell your old John Deere
if you thought the axle was about to go.

I heard the story from a friend of mine,
who heard it from his brother's son-in-law,
who heard it in a country-western bar.
Niobe was her name. She was no Yankee.
Her husband was a banker in New York—
he had a name in Wall Street arbitrage.
They'd bought a Berkshire farm for holidays
and used to stay through August. On Labor Day
they'd roar back to New York in BMWs.
It was the old Mackenzie place—you know it.
Played out for wheat or corn, but decent land
if you wanted just to sit and stare at it.
Slash pine and boulder were its money crop.
She wore the latest fashions from Milan—
a Hermès handbag in the Stop & Shop
when people couldn't pay their mortgages.

Up-mountain lived a woman, the widow L.
The papers still refuse to print her name,
though afterwards they knew just what had happened.
She had the twins, Apollo and Diana.
Even the nurses thought the names were strange;
but the twins were handsome, modest kids—

they stayed up on the farm and did their chores.
The widow L. had a local reputation.
She hadn't been to town in twenty years,
but she was kind to some—sent down preserves,
a rhubarb pie if your husband was laid up.
She always sent a pie down for a funeral.
She wasn't a woman whom you dared to cross—
she had another sort of reputation.
No one hunted deer along that mountain.
They didn't take to strangers on the mountain.

Some other time, and nothing might have happened.
Some other place, and nothing would have happened.
Niobe never learned the country way—
she had a mouth, they say, looking for trouble.
Her mother's father was a nouveau riche,
her father a distinguished senator—
some folks had read about her in the *Bee*.
She had it all—a brownstone off Park Avenue,
a classic face that plastic surgery
could not improve—could not improve much further.
And she had seven sons and seven daughters.
She could have bought and sold that little town,
but she never understood how local folk
could talk about a woman they never saw,
and folks did talk about the mountain widow
as if she were a part-time village saint.
Perhaps it wasn't worship, not exactly,
not like the worship they managed in the church,
but it was, say, close-cousin to such worship.
They liked her better for never having seen her.
Some said she'd been a teenage outcast, hounded
from town to town to have her bastard twins.
Some said that she'd been pregnant by her father.

Now townfolks never cottoned to Niobe.
You had to know her high heels were Italian,
her scarves were French, her rings were Tiffany's.

She was a walking advertisement for free trade.
She knew she had a lot to be grateful for,
but somehow she wanted you to be grateful too.
No wonder she was proud. How could fate touch her?
Even if God had taken a child or two
she owned too much to know what losing was.
If the market crashed, her trusts were well protected;
she had the best investments money could buy,
the best of everything. But not the best of town.
Some people did amend their talk around her,
but she couldn't stop the whispering in private.

One morning in the bank she stood in line
behind two village gossips, who were deep
in some old story about the widow L.
Niobe crossed her arms and then let rip.
'Damned if I'll listen to another word
about this pig-eyed, ignorant mountain girl
who has two bastard twins and welfare checks.
If kids are what you people care about,
how many does she have? A measly two.
Just two. Why, I have seven times as many!
I'm fed up with this ghostly backwoods bitch
who had her little bastards out of wedlock
and bakes you rhubarb pie when you get buried.'

No angry woman was more beautiful,
but there are things you never say aloud
about a stranger's mother. Word got around.
The twins had heard it. They knew what to do.
They dressed up in their hunter's camouflage
though hunting season was a month away,
and took their bows down from the fireplace.
They took a sheaf of arrows barbed for deer . . .

The very youngest was the last to die,
down on his knees in Dr Parker's hay field.
The only thing he said was 'Please don't kill me.'

For a moment, the twins regretted what they'd done,
but the final arrow was already away.
The local folks were stunned. There hadn't been
as many killed in the flood of '34.
The undertaker drove to Boston for the coffins,
but no one said a word against the twins.
It was a justice understood up there.
You don't go looking at that sort of justice.
Some might have called it fate. It wasn't fate.
It wasn't more than what was right. And paid is paid.
Even her enemies had to pity her.
The Wall Street banker? Well, he cut his throat.
Folks thought the better of him after that.
The widow L. sent down a rhubarb pie.

After the funerals, Niobe went insane.
The doctor said she turned as hard as stone.
Some say she really did turn into stone.
Some say her statue's on the mountaintop,
where acid rain erodes its granite face.
Some claim it weeps hot tears, like a wooden Virgin
in some church in Mexico. A miracle.

There *is* a woman's statue on the mountain.
I met some hikers once who said they'd seen it.

The Lycians

PAUL MULDOON

All the more reason, then, that men and women
should go in fear of Leto, their vengeful, vindictive numen,
and worship the mother of Apollo and Artemis
all the more zealously. This last tale of the demise
of Niobe brought others to mind, inspiring no less zeal
among the storytellers. 'On the fertile soil
of Lycia,' one began, 'the peasants, too, would scorn
Leto and pay the price. Since these Lycians were low-born,
the remarkable story of what happened
is scarcely known, though I saw with my own eyes the pond
where the wonder took place. My father, being too frail
to travel far himself, had sent me on the trail
of a string of prime bullocks he'd turned out
in those distant parts. He'd given me a Lycian scout
whom I followed over the rich
pasture till we came on a lake in the midst of which
stood an ancient altar, its stones blackened
by many sacrificial fires, set in a quicken
of reeds. The scout stopped in his tracks and said in a quiet
voice, "Have mercy on us," and I echoed
him, "Have mercy." When I asked my guide
if this was a shrine to the Naiads or Faunus or some such god
he replied, "Not at all, son: no common hill-god or genius
presides over this place but the one whom Juno
sentenced to wander round and round,
never to set foot on solid ground;
the goddess who dwells
here was the one to whom even Delos
gave short shrift,
though Delos itself was totally adrift;
on that unstable island, braced between a palm and a gnarled
olive, she brought her twins into the world,

then, clasping them to her breast,
set off again with Juno in pursuit.
By the time she touched down in Lycia, the bailiwick
of the Chimera, she was completely whacked
from her long travail; the intense heat
had left her drained; her breast-milk had run out.
Just then she stumbled upon a fair-to-middling-sized pond
in which some locals were cutting osiers and bent
and sawgrass and sedge.
Leto knelt by the water's edge
and made to cup her hands. But these local yokels
shook their reaping-hooks and sickles
and wouldn't let her drink. "Why," she begged them, "why
would you deny me what's not yours to deny
since water, along with air and light,
is held by all in common, as a common right?
It's not as if I'm about to throw
myself headlong into your pool. My throat's so dry
and my tongue so swollen I can barely utter
this simple request for a life-giving drink of water.
If not for mine, then for my children's sakes,
I implore you to let us slake
our thirsts." At that moment, the twins stretched
out their little hands. Who could fail to be touched
by such entreaties? These begrudgers, though, were moved
only to renew their threats and foul oaths:
then, to add insult
to injury, they began to stomp about and stir up the silt
on the bottom of the pond, muddying the water
for no reason other than sheer spite.
That was it: that was as much as the Titan's daughter
could take. "Since you've shown," she cried, "no soft spot
for me, in this soft spot you'll always stay."
And stay they have: now they love nothing more than to play
in water, giving themselves over to total
immersion or contentedly skimming the surface: they dawdle
on the bank only to dive back in; now, as ever,
they work themselves into a lather

over some imagined slight; since they continually curse
and swear their voices are hoarse
while their necks, in so far as there's anything between
their heads and shoulders, are goitred; their yellow
paunches set off by backs of olive-green,
they go lepping about the bog-hole with their frog-fellows.'

The Flaying of Marsyas

ROBIN ROBERTSON

nec quicquam nisi vulnus erat
VI, 388

1

A bright clearing. Sun among the leaves,
sifting down to dapple the soft ground, and rest
a gilded bar against the muted flanks of trees.
In the flittering green light the glade
listens in and breathes.

A wooden pail; some pegs, a coil of wire;
a bundle of steel flensing knives.

Spreadeagled between two pines,
hooked at each hoof to the higher branches,
tied to the root by the hands, flagged
as his own white cross,
the satyr Marsyas hangs.

Three stand as honour guard:
two apprentices, one butcher.

2

Let's have a look at you, then.
Bit scrawny for a satyr,
all skin and whipcord, is it?
Soon find out.
So, think you can turn up with your stag-bones
and outplay Lord Apollo?

This'll learn you. Fleece the fucker.
Sternum to groin.
Tickle, does it? Fucking bastard,
coming down here with your dirty ways . . .
Armpit to wrist, both sides.
Chasing our women . . .
Fine cuts round hoof and hand and neck.
Can't even speak the language proper.
Transverse from umbilicus to iliac crest,
half-circling the waist.
Jesus. You fucking stink, you do.
Hock to groin, groin to hock.
That's your inside leg done:
no more rutting for you, cunt.

Now. One of you on each side.
Blade along the bone, find the tendon,
nick it and peel, nice and slow.
A bit of shirt-lifting, now, to purge him,
pull his wool over his eyes
and show him Lord Apollo's rapture;
pelt on one tree, him on another:
the inner man revealed.

3

Red Marsyas. Marsyas *écorché*,
splayed, shucked of his skin
in a tug and rift of tissue;
his birthday suit sloughed
the way a sodden overcoat is eased
off the shoulders and dumped.
All memories of a carnal life
lifted like a bad tattoo,
live bark from the vascular tree:
raw Marsyas unsheathed.

Or dragged from his own wreckage
dressed in red ropes
that plait and twine his trunk
and limbs into true definition,
he assumes the flexed pose of the hero:
the straps and buckles of ligament
glisten and tick on the sculpture
of Marsyas, muscle-man.
Mr Universe displays the map of his body:
the bulbs of high ground carved
by the curve of gully and canal,
the tributaries tight as ivy or the livid vine,
and everywhere, the purling flux of blood
in the land and the swirl of it flooding away.

Or this: the shambles of Marsyas.
The dark chest meat marbled with yellow fat,
his heart like an animal breathing
in its milky envelope,
the viscera a well-packed suitcase
of chitterlings and palpitating tripe.
A man dismantled, a tatterdemalion
torn to steak and rind,
a disappointing pentimento
or the toy that can't be reassembled
by the boy Apollo, raptor, vivisector.

The sail of stretched skin thrills and snaps
in the same breeze that makes his nerves
fire, his bare lungs scream.
Stripped of himself and from his twin:
the stiffening scab and the sticky wound.

Marsyas the martyr, a god's fetish,
hangs from the tree like bad fruit.

Down Under

CIARAN CARSON

1

Then they told the story of the satyr who played the flute
          so brilliantly
In Phrygia, he tried to beat Apollo. Apollo won, of course;
          for extra measure, thought
He'd bring the satyr down another peg or two: stripped
          off his pelt, ungloving it from

Scalpwards down. And could he play then? With his fingertips
          all raw,
His everything all peeled and skinless? You saw the score
          of veins
Externalized, the palpitating circuits. The polythene-like
          arteries. The pulsing bag
Of guts you'd think might play a tune, if you could bring
          yourself to blow and squeeze it.

2

I flipped the tissue-paper and took in the Christian
          iconography.
Its daguerrotype-like, braille feel. The spiky instruments.
          The pincers.
The man who'd invented the saw had studied the anatomy
          of a
Fish's spine. From bronze he cut the teeth and tried them
          out on a boxwood tree.

That ancient boxwood flute of Greece will haunt him yet.
          Through olive groves

Its purple aura bleats through dark and sheep. The dozing
          shepherd
With his flute abandoned. Wrapped up in his mantle,
          independent, fast asleep.

3

I felt like the raw blob of a baby kangaroo that crawls
          the vertical
Fur of its mother, and falls eventually into the pouch,
          exhaustedly.
As Daedalus was herring-boning feathers into wings, I was
The sticky, thumby wax with which he oozed the quills
          together.

I dropped my red blob on the letter-flap and sunk my
          suddenly embodied
Thumb in it. The message inside was the obverse harp
          on an Irish ha'penny;
Bronze, unstrummable. It was there for someone else to flip.

4

Fletcher cut the nib of a quill with a Stanley knife
          and sliced the palp
Of his finger off. It quivered with its hinge of skin,
          then rivuleted
On the parchment. He didn't know where it was going.
          It obscured
The nice calligraphy that looked definitive: like a
          Proclamation or a Treaty.

In fact, he'd been trying to copy the *Inquit* page off
          the Book
Of Kells, as if it were a series of 'unquotes'. The way

you'd disengage
The lashes of a feather, then try and put them back together.

5

The place was packed with expectant academics, but my
    marking slips
Had flittered away from the text. They'd been *Rizla* papers
    in another
Incarnation, when I'd rolled a smoke between my thumbs
    and fingers, teasing
Out the strands. I waffled on about the stet-detectors
    in the library

Basement, security requirements, conduits, wiring,
    laminates and ducts.
Up above, the floors and stacks and filing systems, the
    elaborate
Machinery of books, where I materialized. I strummed
    their rigid spiny gamut.

6

There's a shelf of *Metamorphoses*. Commentaries. Lives.
    The Mystery of Ovid's
Exile. This is where the Phrygian mode returns, by way
    of an Australian stamp
That's slipped out from the covers, bearing the unlikely-
    looking lyre-shaped
Tail of the lyre-bird. Printed in intaglio, it's playing
    a barcarole.

I think of it as clinker-built, Aeolian, floating down
    the limpid river which—
Said Ovid's people—sprang from all the tears the
    country fauns and nymphs

And shepherds wept in Phrygia, as they mourned their
      friend the fettered satyr.

7

So they tell their stories, of the cruelty of gods and
      words and music.
The fledglings of the lyre-bird's song. Its arrows.
      They stare into
The water—'clearest in that Realme'—and see the
      fishes shingled,

Shivered, scalloped on the pebbles. The arrows of the
      wind upon the water,
Written on the water; rolled like smoke, the fluted
      breath that strolls
At midnight. They gaze into the stream's cold pastoral,
      seeing
Fossil ribs and saws embedded there, the flute player's
      outstretched fingers.

Tereus, Procne, Philomela

DAVID WHEATLEY & JUSTIN QUINN

Now, since the reinforcements had helped Tereus
To victory, his fame had spread all over Thrace.
With so well-heeled a pedigree at stake,
King Pandion saw how ideal a match he'd make:
So Tereus wed Procne. Juno though stayed away
From the wedding. Hymen did the same, and all three
Graces. It was the torch-bearing Furies that set
The marriage-bed, as if for some funeral rite.
A fitting omen of their conjugal love,
An eerie screech-owl sat on their bedroom roof
All night; under which sign their child was got.
All Thrace joined their thanksgiving, as it ought,
Declaring the day of the wedding and that of their son
Itys's birth festivals. So blind are men
To their own good!
            Already through five autumns
Titan had wheeled round the peaceful times,
When Procne coaxed her husband: 'If I have pleased you
Send me to see my sister, or her at least to
Visit me: that she'll go quickly back
You can promise my father. This would make
A precious gift for me.' He launched his ship,
Drove oar and sail right to the port of Cecrop
Until on Piraeus's shore he lit.
When he met her royal father, right hand with right
Was joined. Both wished the other hale of heart.
He had just begun to tell of why he'd fared
To them, his wife's request, her given word
Of her returning quickly, were she allowed—
When Philomela entered, richly clothed,
With richer beauty; as we hear the wild
Nymphs when moving through deep woods described,

If only they were clothed as well as her.
That instant Tereus surged with desire,
Like when ripe grain, dry leaves, or ricks of hay,
Torched with flagrance, explode and flame up high.
She was just cause, but his own appetites
Spurred him also, and since his race loves thrice
As quick, his own and nation's fire flared in him.
Corrupt her servants and her nurse, persuade them,
Or tempt the girl herself with gifts for a queen,
Were his first thoughts. Or rape her outright, then
Defend the bloody act with bloody war.
There was nothing that he wouldn't dare
For this mad passion. His chest scarce held its flames.
He pleaded for his cause in Procne's name,
Now eagerly, impatient of delay.
This passion made him eloquent. That Procne
Was all for her coming, was the point he traded
On, if at times it seemed he overdid it,
Adding tears, as if they were his wife's.
O gods, inside the hearts of men there thrives
Black night! While furthering his shameful plan,
The Thracian king appears a kindly man.
And even Philomela asks for it.
She coaxes her father, winding her arms about
His neck, once more to let her see her sister.
For her good—and against it—she pleads with prayer.
Tereus sees her, feels her in his arms,
Sees her kiss the king whom love disarms,
And all this drives him on, fuel for the fury
Of his passion. As she hugs her father, he
Wishes it were him (he still would lust).
Overjoyed when he relents at last
She thanks her father, and she counts a boon
The very thing which seals both sisters' ruin.

By now Phoebus's labours were almost done,
His horses pawing at heaven's western slopes
Where a feast awaited him with wine in gold cups.

Exhausted, they throw themselves down in peaceful repose.
The king retires too, but to pleasures a little more gross:
Philomela. Recalling each detail, her face,
Her legs, her hands, the rest he fantasizes.
Stoking his self-started fires, he gets no sleep that night.
Next day, the old man was moist-eyed at the thought
Of losing his daughter. Wringing Tereus's hand:
'I know,' he said, 'it's what both daughters want,
And you too, Tereus, dear son. It's all for the best.
You know our bonds: I place her in your trust,
And pray by the gods you guard her with a father's
Love. Send her back soon to relieve my last years!
I grudge each day that she's not here with me.
And, Philomela, if you love me don't stay
Too long. One daughter being gone is quite bad enough!'
With these words and a kiss, he saw her off.
Punctuating each request with a tear
He joined both their right hands to make them swear
To keep all the conditions that he had laid down,
And to remember him to his daughter and grandson.
Hardly able to say goodbye through his sobs
His fears for the future began to outweigh his hopes.
No sooner had Philomela stepped on board ship
And the oars begun to churn their way through the trip
Than a smirking Tereus shouted 'Yes! She's mine!'
Scarcely able to put off his pervert's plan
Much longer, he sized her up like a hungry eagle
Would a hare it's caught watching it wriggle,
Dumped in its eyrie. The captor's cruel gloat
Over his victim says it all: no way out.

The journey done, they landed on the shore
And left the ship. He dragged Pandion's daughter
Off to a hut deep in some ancient wood,
And there she trembled, pale with utter dread.
In tears she now asks where her sister is.
He throws her in, and shouting loud his purpose,
He surmounts the poor abandoned virgin,

Vainly screaming out for Pandion
Or Procne, but mostly for the gods above.
She trembles like a lamb who can't believe
She's safe, thrown off and wounded by a wolf—
A dove with bloodied plumage shaking itself,
Afraid still of the claws that ripped through it.
Tearing at her undone hair, now lucid,
As though in mourning, pulling, beating, palms
Outstretched at last, 'You monstrous savage,' she screams,
'What have you done against my father's orders?
Are you reckless of my sister's love, his tears,
My own virginity and bonds of nuptial?
It's all confused. Now I'm your slut, her rival.
You've married both. She is my enemy.
Traitor! So no crime's left undone: kill me!
I wish you'd done as much before this wrong.
My soul would then be pure as it is young.
If gods can see at all, if gods there be,
If all things have not perished here with me,
You'll pay for this. I'll throw aside my shame,
And tell the world at large your wretched crime,
If given half a chance. And if I'm kept
Imprisoned in this wood, I'll fill its depths
And move the rocks with pity for my story.
The gods will hear it ringing through the sky.'

Her words aroused the brutal tyrant's wrath
And fears alike. Stung into action by both
These goads he drew his sword and grabbed her hair,
Pinned her arms to her back and tied them there.
Hearing the drawn steel, Philomela gladly
Offered her throat for the death she wanted so badly.
What he wanted though was her tongue. Putting a halt
To all its cries to her father, his forceps pulled
It out without mercy. The sheared stump quivered.
The rest twitched on the ground, as if in an effort
To speak, the same way snakes' cut-through tails
Thrash, hoping to coil round their mistresses' heels.

That over with—if you'll believe this—he was ready
To treat his lusts to what was left of her body.
Murderer, he'd the nerve to go home to his wife
With a cock-and-bull accident story and crocodile grief.
The tears must have done it. Procne, believing the whole pack
Of lies, tore her gay robes off and went into black,
Erecting a tomb to the sister she now presumed lost
And offering misguided prayers to a spurious ghost.

The god had journeyed through the year's twelve signs.
What can she do? The guard placed there restrains
All flight, huge walls of stone enclose the hut.
Mute lips cannot accuse. Grief sharpens thought
However, and hard times dispose the mind to scheme.
She hung a Thracian warp across her loom
And on its white wove signs with purple woof
That told the crime. When this was done she gave
It to be brought to Procne by her servant,
Begging with gestures. The woman made the errand
To the queen, not knowing what she carried.
The tyrant's wife unrolled the cloth to read
Her sister's ghastly fate in total silence.
Her grief stanched words. Her tongue could find no sense
That's strong enough to heave out all she felt.
No time for tears. All wrongs and rights were cancelled
As her whole soul bends to the thought of vengeance.

It was the time when all the Thracian matrons
Honoured Bacchus (their rite concealed by darkness,
Around Rhodope the cymbals beat and crash),
She puts on her costume for the frantic night,
And leaves the house equipped to fête the god:
Vines trailing from her hair, a deer-skin slung
About her, and on her shoulder a long spear resting.
Like fire, careering through the woods, with a wake
Of rushing servants, she drives hot on the track.
Procne in her headlong fury mimes
Your madness, Bacchus! Now at last she comes

To the lonely hut and screams the Bacchic cry,
'Euhoe!', breaks down the door and tears her free.
Disguising Philomela as one of the Bacchantes,
She drags her in amazement to the palace.

Recognizing the accursed house she'd been brought to
The horrified girl blanched from tip to toe.
But once inside Procne took off the gear
And hugged her abject sister, who still didn't dare
Return her gaze, thinking that she was to blame
For the mess they were in. Longing to prove that her shame
Was all Tereus's fault, but unable to voice
Her oaths or call on the gods her only choice
Was a mime. But to Procne that was just history.
Dismissing her sister's frailty, 'Don't get teary,'
She said, 'You'd do much better to teach your sword-point
To weep, if a sword's not too good for that fiend!
As for myself, sister, I'm ready for bedlam:
Torching the palace, throwing that scheming hoodlum
Into the blaze, or doing a job on the tongue,
The eyes and the fleshier parts that did you such wrong—
Off with them all! We'll squeeze his guilty soul
Out through a thousand wounds. Our plans can't fail
(Whatever they are!)'
                               And just as she said this,
Sauntering towards her came her eldest, Itys.
She knew then what she'd do. Looking him over
With pitiless eyes, 'You know, you're just like your father,'
She said but said no more, the horrific deed
Taking shape inside her raging head.
But when he came closer, and hugged and kissed his mum,
His arms hooking round her neck, boyishly handsome,
She wept despite herself. Her resolve faltered
As Itys touched her to her very heart.
But when she saw that her determination
Was slipping, she turned away: 'Why does one
Speak love when the other's doomed to lose her tongue?
He says "Mother," but she not "Sister"—something's wrong.

Daughter of Pandion, see your husband now,
A crime to stay with him! You've fallen low!'
Without another word she dragged him off,
Like a tigress dragging a small fawn through the rough.
And when they'd reached a quiet part of the house
He threw open his arms as he read in her brows
His fate, and 'Mother! Mother!' he screamed, and tried
Once more to hug her, but she deftly slid
The knife between his breast and ribs, her face
As calm as if it were a gentle embrace.
That finished him, but Philomela slit
A grin across his throat and then they cut
His body up, still warm, still shuddering with fits.
Some parts in saucepans, and others skewered on spits,
It sizzles. The whole room looks as though it gleets.

Such is the feast to which she invites an unwitting
Tereus. No servants or slaves: strictly seating
For one. Tradition, she tells him. Throned in state
On his antique banquet-chair, he starts to eat,
Gorging whole mouthfuls of his own flesh and blood.
'Where's that boy Itys?' he shouts, unaware how rude
An awakening he's in for. Procne, too *schadenfroh*
To miss such a chance, leans forward to give him a clue.
'Try looking inside.' Goggling madly he calls
A second time for his son. The name hardly falls
From his lips when Philomela, all streaming hair
And blood, just like the last time he saw her—
And right now her tongue could have been put to good use—
Jumps out and throws the boy's head in his face.
The king, upending the table that Procne had laid,
Called the Gorgons in hell to come forth to his aid.
If he could, he'd have torn his breast open and spewed
Out the flesh of his flesh, on which he'd just fed.
Weeping and calling himself his son's own tomb
He runs with drawn sword on the daughters of Pandion.
Seeing them flee you'd think that they'd both sprouted wings;
Which they had. Thus assisted, one of them swings

For the woods and one for the roof. But both get away.
Their feathers are stained with the blood of their crime to this day.
Tereus too, lent wings by his grief and his thirst
For revenge, turns into a bird with a Mohican crest
And a long beak, but no sword. So now you know what
The hoopoe always looks so angry about.

Medea

AMY CLAMPITT

The golden fleece—what it precisely was,
the thing the Minyans' boatload of oarsmen
set off to fetch, heading eastward from Pagasae:
one Phrixus having long before been carried
over sea and land by a miraculous
golden ram to Colchis, where the skin
of that same ram still hung, a trophy waiting
to be plucked—are matters one makes sense of
as one can. Meanwhile, the *Argo*
goes cutting through the waves; we're told of how
the blind seer Phineas was daily preyed on
by Harpies, who snatched at every mouthful, and
fouled the rest with their droppings, until
the Sons of Boreas chased them off; of how
the Argonauts, with Jason as their leader,
having gone through all the hardships of seafaring,
came finally ashore where the river Phasis,
muddy and turbulent, flows into the sea.
At once, then, they sought out King Aeëtes
with their demand to be given the ancient fleece,
the golden fleece of the ram that carried Phrixus,
now hanging glittering from a tree, with a dragon
that never slept coiled underneath to guard it.
The response was not at all surprising: the king
imposed conditions. Whoever claimed the fleece
must first harness a pair of brazen-hooved,
fire-breathing bulls, and with them plow a field
sacred to the martial god; the furrows
must then be seeded, out of a brazen helmet,
with the teeth of vipers, and whatever crop
sprang up must then be harvested. While Jason
stood listening to this, Medea,

daughter of King Aeëtes, listened too,
in a state of agitation so extreme
it worsened with each effort to subdue it.
Some force, something other than herself,
blazed in her; in wonder and dismay, she shrank
from giving the upheaval its usual name.
'A god, no telling which,' she told herself,
'has done this. Why, otherwise, think for a minute
the tasks my father calls for from this stranger,
this beautiful young man, outrageous? But
they are outrageous! Why should I care what happens
to this Jason, whom I never saw
before today, except—' Caught up already
in feverish daydreams of marriage, her reason
arguing that whether Jason died or lived
must be a thing of chance, already jealous of
whatever woman was to share his bed,
Medea now found herself enmired
in scathed misgiving over whatever outcome:
fear of the voyage, were she to elope—
fear of the storm wind, of shipwreck (oh, but
with Jason there to cling to!), followed by
compunction: familial treachery,
the shame of it, was now for her unspeakable.
She saw what was required of her—saw it
so clearly that winged, mischief-making Eros
flew off, seemingly defeated.
                                    At peace,
Medea made her way into a grove
that long had been the secret shrine of Hecate,
patroness of witches, densely thicketed
and dark even by day. Wholly at peace,
all agitation gone, she'd been—until
she saw him standing there, in person
more splendid than she had remembered. Just
as, in a mound of ash, the smallest spark,
fanned by a sudden passing breath, revives,
what had been quenched in her revived: Medea

felt the hot blood rush up, flooding her face.
Eyes fixed, she looked, could not but go on looking
at him. Now he was speaking: Jason,
this stranger, had (unbelievably) her hand in his,
was begging her to help him; this stranger
was pledging to make her his wife. In tears
she groaned out, 'What am I doing? Oh, I see it
all too clearly: desire, not ignorance,
is what misguides me. Sir, having the means
to do it, I will save you. You, in return,
will hold to what you've promised.' And so he swore
to her—swore by the triple goddess of
the grove they stood in, by whatever power
might shelter there; swore by the sun-god
Helius, who fathered Aeëtes, his own
sudden father-in-law-to-be—the sun-
god who sees all; swore by the hope
of living past the dangers that beset him.
And so, believing him, she now brought certain
drugs, taught him the potent formula
for each. He went off jubilant.
                              The dawn
had scarcely dimmed the stars when a huge crowd
began assembling round the field of Mars.
When King Aeëtes, in his purple robe,
sat throned among them, the bulls were seen,
their nostrils snorting fire; the noise
that poured from their hot throats was like a chimney's;
beneath their brazen hooves the ground caught fire.
But Jason, Aeson's son, strode up to them
quite unafraid. Their horns were tipped with iron.
Baleful, they swung their heads, they pawed the ground,
the air filled with their sooty bellowing.
The Argonauts went stark with fear. But Jason,
thanks to Medea—so potent were the drugs
she'd given him—approached the bulls unscathed,
patted their dewlaps, yoked them together,
and drove them, furrowing the hitherto

unbroken earth. The Colchians looked on
astonished; the Minyans broke into cheering. Next,
from the brazen helmet Jason took
the vipers' teeth; they had been steeped in poison
so as, once sown, to soften in the ground.
Now with what sudden metamorphosis,
as when an embryo in the womb acquires
its human aspect, this occurred: a crop
of men sprang up, offspring of earth made pregnant
with that evil seed, each man born armed
and brandishing a spear. The watching Greeks
grew faint with apprehension; Medea too,
for all her power, turned white: a thrill of fear
passed through her body at the sight of Jason
menaced, all those spear-points glittering.
To reinforce the strengths already lent him,
she muttered over all the remaining charms
a witch may call upon. Meanwhile, Jason
raised an enormous rock and sent it smashing
into that threatening mêlée; distracted,
they turned and struck at one another, blindly,
until the field they'd sprung from, the field of Mars,
was littered with their corpses; not one warrior
survived the mayhem. And now Jason's men
rushed forward to embrace their leader—as
Medea longed to, though just then she dared not;
for fear of scandal, she contained herself,
exulting that her craft had served so well,
thanking the dark powers to whom she owed it.
There now remained a further task: by those
same powers to lull with herbs the coiled-up
guardian of the tree from which the fleece
had so long hung untouched: the hideously
fanged and crested dragon, with its flicking
triple tongue, that never slept till now:
till Jason with tranquillizing drugs
soothed those swarthy coils, repeating
three times over the accompanying charms.

These did their work: the huge thing drowsed, then slept,
while Jason made off with the golden fleece,
the prize they'd rowed to Colchis for.
                                        Aboard
the *Argo*, among the hastily assembled
ranks of oarsmen, he brought another prize,
the one whose witchcraft had enabled him
to seize the first. Swiftly, the Minyan crew
launched, rowing westward, and in due course
(not to elaborate) safely came
to harbor at Iolcos.
                    Ashore, the waiting
mothers of the heroes offered thanks,
their sires likewise. Fragrant wood was kindled
on all the altars; a bull with gilded horns
was killed according to the usual
sacrificial custom. But of the elders,
one did not appear—Jason's own father
Aeson, whom age had so worn down, it seemed
his end must come. Jason in dismay
burst out to Medea, 'Oh, my wife,
I know how much I owe you, know it to be
all but incomprehensible: my safety,
my very life I owe to you; but if—
and by yourself you can do anything—
if it were possible, I beg you now
to take from my appointed span, my lifetime,
and so prolong my father's—' He broke off
weeping. Medea's heart was touched; but what
she could not tell her husband, what quite
divided them, was the compunction
that struck her at the thought of her own father,
and of the treachery that had cut her off
from all her kin. What she said was,
'Oh, that would be monstrous! Do not suppose
me capable of making such a transfer:
Hecate, whose powers uphold my own,
would never hear of it. You must not think of

so blasphemous a thing, Jason—you must not.
But as a favor, better than the one
you ask, my craft permits me an attempt,
the threefold deity I call upon permitting,
to prolong your aged father's life
with drugs and other secret means.'

        And so
it came about. Three nights remained before
the waxing moon's horns merged, and the orb was full.
Medea, robed and barefoot, her streaming hair
undone, slipped out alone. In the moon-flooded
world there was no motion but the tremulous
scintillation of the stars. Birds slept,
and beasts, and every human being save herself,
who, with arms raised to those stars, turned round
once, twice, thrice; thrice drenched her head
with flowing water; thrice wailed, then fell
on supplicating knees. She called upon
the night, her powers' repository, and on
the stars whose shimmer, with the moon's,
the day gives way to. Three-headed Hecate (lion,
dog, and mare) as the familiar of all
she undertook, she called upon: 'Goddess,
goddess, come to my aid, sustain my craft;
and you, nurturing Earth, to whom I owe
the secret force of herbs; and you, O winds
and breezes; rivers, lakes, and mountains; spirits
of the wood and of the dark, be with me,
join in my endeavor. At your will,
rivers run back through their astonished banks;
seas calm themselves, or rise again in turmoil,
as I may choose; vapors assemble or
disperse, winds go or come; the viper's throat
bursts open at my bidding; rocks, trees,
whole forests are uprooted, mountains shudder,
tremors rock the earth, and all the spirits
of the buried dead spring from it. I can even—
despite the brazen racket of those devotees

who would forestall eclipse—blot out the moon.
The blazing disk of Helius, the sun-god,
my own grandsire, glows feebly, and the Dawn
turns pale, because of my ensorcellings.
Remember, it was you, you powers, who
for my sake at Colchis, once subdued
the fire-breathing, brazen-footed bulls
that never had been yoked; that drew the plowshare
for my sake; and it was you who guided
that sudden army, sprung out of the ground,
to internecine war; it was through your doing,
lulling the dragon's sleeplessness, that Jason
carried back the golden fleece. I need you
once again. I need the herbs whose juices
can bring a man back out of withered age
into the prime of life. I count on you
to give what I have need for. Not for nothing
have the stars themselves responded; not for nothing
is the chariot I see approaching
hitched to a team of dragons!'
                                        As soon as
the car was at her side, she stepped aboard
and, stroking the bridled pair, shook out
the reins. Soon, airborne, she looked down
on Tempe in Thessaly, knowing precisely where
the search would take her: to the slopes of Ossa
for certain plants, to Pelion and Othrys,
to Pindus and high Olympus for others.
Some she plucked up by the roots, some she cut
with a blade of bronze. She found many
to her liking on Apidanus' banks,
those of Amphrysus, and Enipeus,
Peneus, Spercheus, and Boebe's reedy shore;
Anthedon, near the island of Euboea,
whose virtue Glaucus, having tasted of it
and become immortal, would one day give fame to.
Nine days and nights aboard that car, upborne
by dragon wings, the search continued.

And now, having inhaled a pungent whiff of
the witch's harvest, her scaly carriers
sloughed the skin of age. And now, before
her own threshold, she halted; for no man
might touch her, or see her work. Two altars,
one on her right to Hecate, the other
to Youth, she built of turf, and heaped them both
with branches from the wood. By each of these
she dug a trench, into which blood flowed
from the slit throats of two black rams.
Now she poured in, by the cupful, wine
and foaming milk, meanwhile calling out
her incantations—calling on Pluto, and
the wife he stole to rule with him in hell, and
every earthly spirit, to forbear
from zeal to snatch Aeson's life away.
Assured at length that all these powers were in
accord with what she pleaded for, she now
summoned her husband: and now Aeson's
decrepit frame was carried from the house.
On the hard ground before the altars, eased
by a bed of herbs, he lay, and while
the witch resumed her incantations, sank
in slumber so profound he seemed indeed
to be a corpse. And now she ordered
Jason and his attendants to stand back
from rites they might not know the nature of.
Quickly they were gone. Medea then,
wild-haired as any follower of Bacchus,
circled the altars she had set afire,
then dipped a pair of deeply cloven torches
into the pit she'd filled with blood; when both
had been well drenched, she set them to burn
on the by now crackling altars. Thrice
she purged with fire the body of Aeson, then
with water and then brimstone. Now to the brew
that frothed and bubbled with mingled juices
from all the herbs she'd gathered in her airborne

tour of Thessaly—to these she added
gemstones from the east, and gravel from the shores
far to the west, along with hoar-frost
lately collected, a screech-owl's corpse,
the innards of a werewolf, that horridly
can change into a man. Nor was this all:
it had in it the sloughed-off skins of certain
Lydian water-snakes; also the liver
of a stag, that reaches a great age,
and also from the Methuselah
of crows she took the head and beak; nor were
these all that went into the pot she drew from
to work her awesome purpose. As she stirred
the stuff, the dried-up branch of olive
she stirred it with turned green; soon, leaves
appeared; the silvery, clustering, rounded fruit
grew heavy; and now, wherever the bubbling froth
spilled over, tender grass appeared, a foam
of bloom sprang up at once. Medea,
seeing this, knew it was time. Now, with
a sharpened blade she opened Aeson's throat.
The blood poured; when his veins and arteries
were emptied, she refilled his frame
both at the mouth and through the wounded throat,
with her black medicine. At once
the age-whitened hair and beard of Aeson
turned dark again; the ashen
decrepitude was gone, his wrinkles vanished;
once more young and muscular, Aeson
woke changed into another man—the one
of forty years before.
                    Now from Olympian
heights Bacchus had seen all this, and for
his withered nurses begged of Medea a like
rejuvenation. Having given it,
she neither could nor would leave off
the mischief of her craft. Feigning a rift
with Jason, at the court of Pelias, who'd

usurped Aeson his brother, she meekly
sought asylum. Telling of how she'd conjured
not only Jason's safe return from Colchis,
but also Aeson from decrepitude
to vigorous youth, in Pelias's daughters
her make-believe aroused such eagerness
by the same trickery to see his life
extended, she need only name her price.
She seemed judiciously to hesitate;
then said, 'As proof of my sincerity,
bring me the oldest, feeblest ram you own,
and let me turn it back into a lamb.'
And so a much-enfeebled animal, with horns
the years had massively coiled and incurved,
was brought. At once the sorceress's blade
was at its throat, the thin blood flowed, and in
a pot where chosen herbs were simmering
she plunged the carcass. The lean limbs shrank,
the craggy horns fell off; in the next instant
bleatings from inside the pot were heard.
While the onlookers stared, a lamb jumped out
and ran off looking for a dug to suck.
Awestruck, the daughters of King Pelias
begged Medea still more urgently
to do as she had promised.
                        Three times
the sun-god had unyoked the blazing horses
that each night, out past the coast of Spain,
plunge into the west; and on the fourth,
after the stars appeared, Aeëtes' daughter
went treacherously to work. Though in the pot
she now set boiling there were herbs, they were
herbs with no magic force. King Pelias
and his attendants meanwhile slept deep; Medea
had seen to that. Urging his daughters,
who stood about his bed, she taunted them,
'Why do you hesitate? Quick now, with
those blades of yours, let out his feeble blood,

so with the blood of youth I may replace it.
His life is in your hands. If you care for him
truly, prove it: with those weapons
dispatch his old age, let the blood flow.'
The daughters of Pelias, thus challenged,
performed the deed they shrank from, solely
in the belief that not to have performed it
was wrongful. Not one of them could look
at what she did, but only struck out blindly,
repeatedly, till the bewildered king,
blood-drenched and mutilated, rose to one elbow,
gasping, 'What is this? My daughters,
what are you doing? Who drove you to it?'
And now his daughters' resolution left them;
Medea it was who cut his words short
and slit his throat. Leaving the mangled
corpse to simmer uselessly, the witch took off,
quickly dragon-airborne—otherwise
there would surely have been retribution—
high over Pelion, over Ophrys, over
Aeolian Pitane and the grove of Ida.
And still she flew; scene after vivid scene
passed underneath that car, until at length
she made a halt at Corinth—where, it's said,
the human shape first showed itself, rain-nourished,
metamorphosed from mushrooms.
                                        Years passed;
rejoined by Jason, the sight of whom had so
transformed her life, she lived there with him;
gave birth to sons; and then, enraged
by Jason's infidelity, killed them
outright, and deviously set fire to
his intended bride. A fugitive
once more, she called on her winged beasts, sprung
from the stock of Titans, and flew straight to
the city of Athena, where King Aegeus
(the story goes on being awful), to be brief,
made the mistake of making her his wife.

The Plague at Aegina

JAMES LASDUN

Cephalus at Aegina, not a face
Familiar on the skiffs or landing place;
With a discreet glance round he notes their features:
Hard, thin-lipped, pallid. 'Aeacus, these creatures
Milling in silence on the quays seem . . . odd,
Not quite, if you'll permit me, flesh and blood;
Pin-pupilled as if flushed from underground,
And this eerie silence! Not a human sound;
No cheer, no cry of greeting, not a voice
Raised for my ships . . . Where are they now, the boys
Who ran with me before through the game-crammed woods
With slings and javelins, young men built like gods,
And the women, Aeacus, with sparkling eyes
Who kept me company at the sacrifice,
Soft laughter on their lips as they threw the garlands
Into the embers forging our alliance,
Where are they now? And the clowns, the leopard tamers,
Dancers and jugglers who matched me at our famous
Revels drink for drink till the sun came up
Firing the sands like wine spilt from a cup?'
To which Aeacus with the abrupt frown
Of one whom the memory of loss casts down
As bleakly as the loss itself, replied,
'In their graves, Cephalus; our kingdom's pride
Trampled like ripening cornstalks by some vague
Vaporous army . . . Cephalus, a plague
Was granted us by the gods; a pestilence
That made an equal mockery of science
And prayer. No hope was left us but the hope
Of a quick death . . . Look, where the forests slope
Down from the mountains; there—some say from the spite
Of Jove's spurned jealous goddess at the sight

Merely of shadow-seeking human love
Minding its business in a quiet grove—
The disease began. From there it spread to town
Where like an artist coming into his own
It turned prolific, spewing its singular species
Of sculpture by the cartload; masterpieces
Of corpsework, moulding its sumptuous cadavers
Out of prime flesh—young warriors, athletes, lovers;
First it blew on their innards like a coal
Till their skin flushed and sweat began to roll
Profusely from every pore, then swelled their tongues
And set a racking spasm in their lungs
So that each difficult breath came like the knife
Of a skilled torturer prolonging life
Only to lengthen pain. Meanwhile its brush
Stippled black sores across the burning flesh
Till even the softest linen seemed to scour,
And victims writhed face downward on the floor
As if intent on hastening their own
Reunion with the nerveless realm of stone.
Then, Cephalus, their suffering began;
A kind of teeming numbness overran
Their senses: hearing, taste, smell, touch, then sight,
Eclipsing till unmitigated night
Gripped them, and then came madness, the mind's own
Catabolic horrors, mushroom-grown
In the putrescence of itself . . . Great dismal
Moth wings flapping in the skull, phantasmal
Demons with scourges . . .' Here the king broke off,
Staring a moment at his guest. 'Enough.
Suffice it that death was welcome when it came
Though the disease still sputtered like a flame
In the dead corpse, and just as before their ends
The sick infected doctors, family, friends,
So the dead also laboured in the slaughter,
Seeping the sickness out into earth and water,
Coiling it into the air like rotting meat
As their piled-up bodies mounted in the street

Too fast for us to bury them . . . Each breath
Seemed a deliberate overture to death;
Every drop of water or crumb of bread
Weighed on the tongue like coins the already dead
Bring for the ferryman, a living hand
Brushed in passing seared one like a brand
With terror of death . . . How could we not despair,
Those of us still living, when the mere
Fact of being human was like a crime
Punishable by torture at the whim
Of a capricious tyrant? Some attempted
To outmanoeuvre fate by suicide:
Afflicted logic. Others gave away
All they possessed and left their homes to pray
For mercy in the temples, where they died:
Congregations of corpses side by side
As ineffectual then in dumb reproach
As in loud pious prayer before. Soon each
Citizen withdrew into a dull
Apathy, or best a cynical
Contempt for life, for all that promised once
Superabundant pleasure to every sense,
For what in their own flesh once used to surge
Obediently at life's replicating urge—
Mantis rapture in which our bodies swim
A moment till it rips us limb from limb . . .
So our survivors crept through the mausoleum
Our once convivial island had become;
Frightened, shunning each other as they drifted
Past silent buildings, ghostlier than the dead;
Too few of us, and those too young or old
To till the neglected fields, hunt deer, rebuild
Houses on unpolluted land, clean wells,
Or grind our scavenged corn at the rusting mills,
So that those plague had spared now seemed condemned
To die of cold or hunger, the whole race doomed!
For what? What sin, what crime against the gods
Could merit that?

'One evening in the woods
(The same you spoke of, Cephalus, where you hunted
With the young men I gave you, all since dead),
While searching for birds' eggs like the humblest
Of my own subjects, reaching for a nest
In an old oak, I saw a moving column
Of ants returning up a twisting limb
Into the hollow trunk. Some carried grains
Twice their own size, some linked in living chains
Round battling moths or beetles that others dragged
Homeward like enemy hostages. None lagged
Or idled on the march—if empty-jawed
They formed impromptu regiments and warred
On other stray rivals or helped a neighbour;
Thousands of them, teeming in silent labour
Along the furrowed ridges . . . I who'd lost
As many people, watched this swarming host
In a strange dream-like anguish . . . Falling down
Onto my knees, I cried out, "Father of Heaven,
Maker of earth and sky and all that lives,
You whom this fanatic order gives
Less offence, it seems, than our own human
Muddle of blind desire and fumbling vision,
Grant me people like these, since you favour them,
And in such numbers; fill my empty kingdom
With a new race of men."
                                   'At once the tree's
Branches started to shake, though not a breeze
Disturbed the air. I felt my own limbs tremble,
My hair rise as the ants began to tumble
Onto the ground beside me where they raised
Their armoured bodies up. I watched amazed
As inch by inch they grew before my eyes:
Hind legs stretching and swelling to human size,
Heads bulging, torsos bloating out to burnished
Breastplates, mid-limbs shrinking till they vanished,
And in the shape of men they filled the woods
Silently in massed ranks spreading backwards

Far as the eye could see. Then each one raising
A new-formed arm, they hailed me as their king.

'These are the men and women, Cephalus,
You see before you now; my insect race,
Just as I'd asked for in my prayer to Jove.
As you might guess from my description, Love,
That once amused us with its faithful cast
Of fluttering Crushes, over-perfumed Lust,
Passion's soprano foghorn wailing in vain
At Vanity, Suspicion with his pain,
Hasn't found great favour with these creatures,
And though this touch of coldness in their natures
Is more than balanced by their loyalty,
No king was ever more estranged than I
From his own populace. But let that pass.
They're thrifty, disciplined, industrious,
Brutal in battle. I call them Myrmidons
In memory of their milling origins.
They'll follow you obediently in the wars
Our treaty binds us in. Take them, they're yours.'

Scylla and Minos

MICHAEL HOFMANN

I knew about Helen, they kept selling me Helen,
but I never even got to be stolen in the first place.
Sieges are boring—did you know. Everything's fine,
just each day's a little bit worse than the last.

And you start thinking how long it is since you saw
prawns or a nice pair of earrings or a magazine.
I had my townhouse, but I practically lived on the battlements,
they even let me use the telescope during the lulls.

Then one day I saw him. That changed everything.
Oiled limbs, greaves (can you imagine), his little skirt,
roaring and rampaging about, the bellowed (yes, taurean) commands.
By Jupiter out of Europa, apparently. I thought: gimme!

A big girl wants a man like that, not the little weasels
scurrying around defending me. (Did I ask to be defended?)
I started cheering him on as he skewered our guys.
I wondered if he could see me and what he thought.

Was he stuffing a goat, hitting the 3 star, or letters home.
Minos, Minos King of Crete. I tried on a Cretan accent,
did that all the hair up all the hair down thing they do there.
I thought of the word Argive—or were we the Argives?

Perhaps if we lost—and how could we fail to lose,
how could anyone hold out against him, he's so irresistible—
then I'd get to be his wife or his sex slave or something.
Who cares, frankly. Isn't that what happens. After a war?

That's when I started thinking about trying to help things along.
Not pushing 'our boys' over the edge, or distracting them from the job
    in hand
by giving them blow jobs as they manned the walls (man something else),
something more ruthless, I suppose, and more wholesale.

I wrote to Minos, signed 'a fan', to meet me at the gate.
It wasn't easy, believe me. At night I spiked their drinks.
I went into Daddy's bedroom with the garden shears
and cut off his purple scalplock. The creepy thing went and bled on me.

There. I shouldn't have told you. Anyway, I popped it in a bag
and ran to the Maidens' Gate. He wasn't there of course.
So I had to pick my way through his dreaming army
with it in my hands, by now it was hissing softly.

He was up, of course (so conscientious!),
in something skimpy, bustling about his tent,
wet jockstraps hanging up to dry. (What I'd give!)
The funny thing is he didn't seem pleased to see me, I looked.

I said: This is the purple hair of Nisus.
The siege is over. Invest the town. (Invest me!)
He got all huffy, gave me stuff about war and men and honour,
said something so underhand had no place in the annals, etc.,

and no way was I ever going to Crete at his side.
I said did he like war so much, he didn't want it to end.
The next day his flag was flying over Megara
and they were loading the ships.

He dictated peace terms. My father abdicated.
I stumbled about the campsite, thinking what I'd done,
what there was for me to do. I couldn't go back,
and which of the other towns on the strip would have me—

like giving houseroom to the Trojan horse,
the Trojan bicycle more like. It was Crete or nothing.

He stood by the mast, arms crossed, for all the world like Ulysses.
I said: Fuck you, Minos, your wife does it with bulls!

Then I saw my father coming for me, he was an osprey,
he was rejuvenated, I gave a little mew of terror,
and found myself flying too, criss-crossing the sea,
Scylla the scissor-legged, now the shearer.

Perdix

MICHAEL LONGLEY

In the wings of that story about the failure of wings
—Broken wings, wings melting, feathers on water, Icarus—
The garrulous partridge crows happily from a sheugh
And claps its wings, a hitherto unheard-of species,
The latest creation, a grim reminder to Daedalus
—Inventor, failure's father—of his apprentice, a boy
Who had as a twelve-year-old the mental capacity
To look at the backbone of a fish and invent the saw
By cutting teeth in a metal blade; to draw conclusions
And a circle with the first compass, two iron limbs,
Arms, legs tied together, geometry's elbow or knee—

Which proved his downfall, for Daedalus grew so jealous
He pushed the prodigy headlong off the Acropolis
And then fibbed about him slipping; but Pallas Athene,
Who supports the ingenious, intercepted his fall,
Dressed him in feathers in mid-air and made him a bird,
Intelligence flashing to wing-tip and claw, his name
Passing on to the bird (it is *perdix* in the Greek)—
The partridge that avoids getting airborne and nesting
In tree-tops or on dizzy ledges; that, flapping along
At ground level, laying its eggs under hedges, has lost,
Thanks to the memory of that tumble, its head for heights.

The Log of Meleager's Life

MICHAEL HOFMANN

The woman who gave you life, put her hand,
her whole body, into the fire for you,
pulled you out, red-blue, bald and blistered,
remembers the agony with every candle on your cake—
what if she'd the right to return you
to non-being for something you'd said or done,
or just calling in a debt, to stand there
at either end of your life like Kafka's doorman:
judge and jury, while you burn (baby) in ignorance?

Achelow and Pamela

KARL KIRCHWEY

It was a hog run wild in a neighboring town
that first took Fazius away and brought him back again,

in this case feeling rather low-spirited,
because his own best shot had been obstructed

by a leafy branch, his good old boy's composure
already shaken by Atlanta, and Milagro's crush on her.

But the river was in flood, barges idled for miles
in both directions, bridges washed out up past Nichols,

so when he saw the sign: DON'T CROSS THE RIVER DRY!
STOP AT ACHELOW'S, he stopped in immediately

to watch the river and listen to the talk
while he nursed a Flood Special (93-cent beer, domestic).

And what he heard was, 'I saw cows in it, back in '51,
but this time a deer on a chunk of levee broken

off like an island.' 'That's nothing. I saw burial vaults
floated into the tree line like so many cedar closets.'

'I saw what happened when the river got a grip
on a storage tank—crushed it like a foam coffee cup.'

'And you heard about that laser artist up at K.C.?
Fell out of his studio and drowned. What's a laser artist, exactly?'

Fazius noticed it was an odd grotto of a bar,
the carpeting gone mossy, a riverine humidor,

and the ceiling spangled with glass bits and purple shells,
conches and trash encrusting the cinderblock walls,

souvenirs brought back over time, apparently,
from Disney World vacations by the proprietor and his family.

Fazius looked out over the muddy currents
and said, 'Is that one island I see, or five islands?'

And Achelow, his voice a series of eddies and glides,
said, 'I call what you see there the I-Can-Adds:

flood insurance, friend. Each one not an island but a home,
reduced by the waters to a pile of flotsam.

Why, I myself have five daughters living upriver.
God forbid these should be their houses (not that they've ever

shown me the least gratitude, not a single one)
but now their places—Orrick, West Alton, Richmond, Hardin,

and Rhineland—are washed out or glazed over with the dregs
of the river or are crawling all over with little green frogs.

Sure I'll help them out. What is it the old poet says?
Something like "Divisions are hid by distances."

But let me tell you, when I see Nature, bit in her teeth,
seven million gallons a minute and cornfields underneath,

the highways like oyster crackers floating on soup,
the river that was once two miles away now lapping your doorstep

impatiently, when I see berms cave in and sand boils
churning, why then I think the river knows just how it feels

to have daughters who don't keep in touch.' It's five football fields wide
now; there's summer training on the cable TV overhead.

Fazius wonders how he will get home. Achelow has begun,
in that whispering voice of his, to tell stories again,

and Fazius' two other companions at the bar—
the unlikely-named Lilacs, a streak of gray in his hair,

and skinny Prothero, too cocky and with quite a mouth
on him—are already eyeing an empty booth;

yet he is their host, and so they do not move.
'In fact, I owe meeting my late wife (may she live

in memory) to the '51 flood. She was fishing perch
or a line of catfish from the tarpaper roof of her porch,

I remember, when I hitched my rowboat to a phone pole
and invited her to come play mud volleyball.

The weather man calls it a blocking pattern, rain stalled over us,
but that day we sure weren't blocked. The game got kind of loose,

on that island just over there, shaped like—well, like the hip
and bosom of a woman, half-wooded and half-steep,

and me and Pamela snuck off together alone.
Now, you know what gossip's like in a small town,

and her old man, who was so fat the neighbor kids knew
him as "Hippo'tamus", got mad and threw

her out of the family house down on Water Street.
"Achelow," she said, "my own father's called me a slut.

You've got to help me, because I've got no place to go.
Give me a place, make me a place, make a place for me, Achelow."

I touched her shoulder—she was all over quivering—
feeling sandbagged at first, but I did the right thing,

and I said to her, "You were born and baptized here,
and we're never going to live anywhere but by this river."

So we did, and raised five children, till her death in March.
But I named the place Pamela's Island, after the touch

I first knew her by, and that's the name it'll go
by always around here, whether flood or no.'

There was a thoughtful silence, this time, and no shifting
of barstools, except that Prothero was snickering.

But Lilacs cut him with a sharp look and he was still;
for Lilacs had his own country ballad to tell.

Baucis and Philemon

MICHAEL LONGLEY

In the Phrygian hills an oak tree grows beside a lime tree
And a low wall encloses them. Not far away lies bogland.
I have seen the spot myself. It should convince you
—If you need to be convinced—that the power of heaven
Is unlimited, that whatever the gods desire gets done.

Where a drowned valley makes a sanctuary for water birds
(Divers, coots), a whole community used to plough—until
Jupiter brought Mercury without his wand or wings.
Disguised as humans, they knocked at a thousand houses
Looking for lodgings. A thousand houses slammed the door.

But one house took them in, a cottage thatched with straw
And reeds from the bog. Baucis and Philemon, a kindly
Old couple, had been married there when they were young
And, growing old together there, found peace of mind
By owning up to their poverty and making light of it.

Pointless to look for masters or servants here because
Wife and husband served and ruled the household equally.
So, when these sky-dwellers appeared at their cottage-home
Stooping under the low door to get in, the old man
Brought them stools to sit on, the old woman cushions.

She raked the warm ashes to one side and fanned into life
Yesterday's embers which she fed with leaves and dry bark,
The breath from her old body puffing them into flames.
She hoked around in the roof-space for twigs and firewood,
Broke them up and poked the kindling under her skillet.

She took the cabbage which Philemon had brought her
From the garden plot, and lopped off the outer leaves. He

Lowered a flitch of smoked bacon from the sooty rafters
And carved a reasonable helping from their precious pork
Which he simmered in bubbling water to make a stew.

They chatted to pass the time for their hungry visitors
And poured into a beechwood bucket dangling from its peg
Warm water so that the immortals might freshen up.
Over a sofa, its feet and frame carved out of willow,
Drooped a mattress lumpy with sedge-grass from the river.

On this they spread a coverlet, and the gods sat down.
The old woman tucked up her skirts and with shaky hands
Placed the table in front of them. Because one leg was short
She improvised a wedge and made the surface level
Before wiping it over with a sprig of water-mint.

She put on the table speckly olives and wild cherries
Pickled in wine, endives, radishes, cottage-cheese and eggs
Gently cooked in cooling ashes, all served on crockery.
Next, she produced the hand-decorated wine-jug
And beechwood cups polished inside with yellow wax.

In no time meat arrived from the fireplace piping hot
And the wine, a rough and ready vintage, went the rounds
Until they cleared the table for a second course—nuts
And figs and wrinkly dates, plums and sweet-smelling apples
In a wicker basket, purple grapes fresh from the vines.

The centrepiece was a honeycomb oozing clear honey,
And, over everything, the circle of convivial faces
And the bustle of hospitality. And then the hosts
Noticed that the wine-jug, as soon as it was emptied,
Filled itself up again—an inexhaustible supply.

This looked like a miracle to Philemon and Baucis
Who, waving their hands about as if in prayer or shock,
Apologized for their home-cooking and simple recipes.
They had just one gander, guardian of the smallholding,
Whom they wanted to sacrifice for the divinities.

But he was too nippy for them and flapped out of danger
Into the immortals' arms. 'Don't kill the goose!' they thundered.
'We're gods. Your tightfisted neighbours are about to get
What they deserve. You two are granted immunity.
Abandon your home and climb the mountainside with us.'

Unsteady on their walking-sticks they struggled up the steep
Slope and glancing back, a stone's throw from the top, they saw
The townland flooded, with just their homestead high and dry.
While they stood flabbergasted, crying out for neighbours,
Their cottage (a squeeze for the two of them) became a church.

Stone pillars took the place of the home-made wooden piles,
The thatching glowed so yellow that the roof looked golden,
Filigree transformed the doorway, and marble tiling
Improved the dirt floor. Jupiter spoke like a gentleman:
'Grandpa, if you and your good wife could have one wish . . . ?'

'May we work as vergers in your chapel, and, since our lives
Have been spent together, please may we die together,
The two of us at the one time? I don't want to see
My wife buried or be buried by her.' Their wish came true
And up to the last moment they looked after the chapel.

At the end of their days when they were very old and bowed
And living on their memories, outside the chapel door
Baucis who was leafy too watched Philemon sprouting leaves.
As tree-tops overgrew their smiles they called in unison
'Goodbye, my dear'. Then the bark knitted and hid their lips.

Two trees are grafted together where their two bodies stood.
I add my flowers to bouquets in the branches by saying

'Treat those whom God loves as your local gods—a blackthorn
Or a standing stone. Take care of caretakers and watch
Over the nightwatchman and the nightwatchman's wife.'

Erisychthon

JAMES LASDUN

1

The scene: a town under mountains;
Clapboard, shingle and brick, the usual
Straggle of shopping malls, post-colonial
Factory outlets and fast-food chains
Thinning upward through scant
Cattle pastures then woods
Where the hulk of a disused chemical plant

Drips and leaks. This was built by one
Erisychthon, who as it happens
Also built the malls and the fast-food chains,
Outlets too—in fact who'd built the town,
Downtown at least; who owned
A piece of everything,
And several pieces of the board who'd zoned

Or rather rezoned certain lands
Once listed 'Grade A Conservation'
As 'Grade E, Suitable for Speculation',
Placing in their benefactor's hands
The local beauty spots
Which he, magician-like,
Tore to pieces and turned into parking lots,

Malls, outlets, chains, et cetera.
This is our hero, Erisychthon;
Ex-boxer, self-styled entrepreneur, ex-con
(Wire fraud, two years in a white-collar
'Country Club') after which

The town received him back
With open arms. Why not? He'd made them rich,

Some of them anyway, besides
He had a certain big man's swagger
People admire; a cross between an ogre
And Father Christmas: three hundred pounds,
Bearded, built like a vat,
With a great booming voice
And a cuff on the chin that could knock you flat.

He and his daughter, a shy girl
Who doted on him in a perverse
Return for his neglect, abuse or worse,
Lived in a ramshackle gothic pile
With its own pool and grounds
Planned by himself, put up
By his own men, and just as he cheated friends,

So he'd managed to cheat himself:
Cheap timbers warping, shoddy brickwork
Damp on the plastered insides, outside a murk
Of crooked-lined mortar; not a shelf,
Door or cupboard nailed straight,
The skimped-on pipes bursting
Every winter . . . Yet over this second-rate

Botched-up construction seemed to float
A yearning, an almost palpable
Dream of grandeur and splendour, of epic scale—
Vintage cars on the drive, a powerboat
Dry-docked in the garage,
Barbecues big enough
For hogs and oxes on the tilting acreage

Of the rear porch: pure appetite
So strong at first glance it seemed to change

Will into deed, so that briefly by a strange
Hypnotism you transformed the sight
Into its own ideal,
Pinnaced and shimmering,
As if he'd tripped you up on some hidden zeal

You yourself harboured for excess . . .
This was his secret; to sell his clients
On their own luck-rich dreams. The plant for instance
(Electrolyte for capacitors)—
He'd lured the company
Less by the usual talk
Of tax breaks, kickbacks, et cetera, than by

Some potent, invisible
Spume of unlimited confidence
That reached them from his squat bulk like the hormones
By which certain animals compel
Others to roll over
And get shafted, which was
Precisely what they did. Within a year

The concrete floor had fissured. Waste
Seeped through the cracks. Teratogenic
(Lit.: 'monster-breeding') PCBs and toxic
Potions to suit every other taste
Were found in a nearby
Spring-fed pool where hunters
Told of seeing at twilight an unearthly

Fluorescence in the reeds, of strange
Deformities in local creatures
Web-footed mice, snakes with fur in patches,
Dropped antlers with a bluish mineral tinge . . .
True or not, the place shut
And for a while our man
Was banned from the trade. But genius will out,

And in his retreat from the world
(This was how he preferred to term it)
He had a vision, as befits a hermit:
Before him a spread of trees unfurled—
A radiant, flower-filled wood
With a clearing in which
Clusters of brand-new sunshot houses stood.

Luxury homes; but more than just
Luxurious (and this is what we mean
By genius); he'd design the whole thing green!
What? Erisychthon turned ecologist?
Apparently. No scam
Surely could bring such pious
Tears to his eyes; 'I'm green, I really am,'

He said out loud as a swell
Of righteousness filled his heart: 'I'll build
Windmills and solar panels, use recycled
Paper for prospectuses, and sell
Not houses but ideals
Carved in organic forms
From eco-friendly natural materials . . .

Let's say a million bucks apiece
Which isn't much considering
How good you'll feel just living there and saving
The earth, in fact it's cheap at the price.'
So to the zoning board
Whose members could be seen
Later that year at choice resorts abroad

Sunning themselves, expenses paid.
Then to the S & L, a boardroom lunch
To pitch for funds: 'My friends I have a hunch
That one day on our children's lips *Cascade*'—
(His name for the project)

—'Will be a word for hope;
A word for how we didn't self-destruct,

A word for courage, for the best
In our great nation under God, the true
Spirit of enterprise, get-up-and-go, can-do;
Call me a bleeding heart, an idealist,
Call me a renegade
Liberal, but, my friends,
I have a hunch that history wants Cascade—

I have a hunch that one day we
Who built it will have built a paradise
Sung with our fruited plains and spacious skies
Praised with our purple mountains' majesty . . .'
And so on till the air
Filled with directors' sobs.
'We're in,' they cried, 'we're green, we really are.'

2

High above town a first-growth wood
Fanned out from a crease in the mountain
Where waterfalls churned a mist like pile-driven
Marble dust; a sparkling quarry cloud
On which a rainbow played.
This was the lucky site
Our hero had selected for Cascade,

Though to a certain sect in town,
Keepers of a certain mystic flame,
The wood had long been known by another name:
The *White and Blue*. In spring the waving crown
Of dogwood and hawthorn trees
Formed a white cumulus
Of blossom above, while like a tapestry's

Millefleur background, an undergrowth
Of cream-coloured wildflowers spread below—
Featherbells, sweet white violets, moonseed, yarrow,
Trembling wood-anemones—till the earth
Foamed like a breaking wave
With living surf. And then,
As spring passed, blue, the blue of a chapel nave

Under a blue rose-window rose
Like a blue-blooded blush into the white;
Wild hyacinth, hyssop skullcap, aconite,
Blooming over the ground while buckthorn sloes
And juniper berries
Hung ripening above.
Here our sect, a sisterhood of Ceres—

White witches mostly—assorted
Healers, herbalists and hierophants
Of Wicca—came each month to gather plants:
Cohosh, lobelia roots, enchanter's nightshade,
White milkweed for the heart,
Emetic gentian; raw
Matter for every magic or mystic art.

Needless to say the *White and Blue*
Was precious to them, and when the word
Of Cascade reached their ears, they flew to the wood,
Arriving just as Erisychthon's crew
Were unloading chainsaws.
Circling a central stand
Of ancient trees, they cried, 'This wood is ours,

'Sacred to our goddess: touch it
And our curse be on your heads.' The crew
Hung back: in this uncertain era few
Had quite the rashness not to admit
At least a vague belief

In most things spiritual—
Curses, auras, Atlantis, an afterlife

On other planets; however,
Our hero, drunk on his rhetoric,
Had lathered up an almost messianic
Zeal for his project, and a quiver
Of indignation shook
His great bulk as he learned
Of this pious protest. Jumping in his truck

And barrelling up to the wood,
Where he found the women hand in hand
Stalling his men, he bellowed: 'This is my land,
Let me get at those trees or you're as good
As lumber yourselves. I paid'—
(Grabbing a chainsaw here)
—'My money, now I've come to build Cascade.'

And holding out the saw, he strode
Towards the protestors. One of them,
A grey-haired, soft-spoken woman by the name
of Gendenwitha (Iroquois word
For Day Star), gently stepped
Out of the ring and spoke
Of her own ancestors who'd worshipped

In this very spot; of how each
Tree was once thought to contain a soul
'So that to chop—' but with a contemptuous snarl
Erisychthon cut her off mid-speech,
Giving the starter cord
Of his chainsaw a yank,
And revving the engine till the big blade roared

Violently into life; and so,
Wielding it wildly in front of him,
He cut through an iron-hard hornbeam, lopped each limb

Of an oak from its trunk, and as though
The mutilated stump
Woke some demon in him,
He rampaged through the wood; slashed out at a clump

Of hazels that leapt like soldiers
Blown from a trench . . . Pines and birches fell
Under the swipe of his blade, a sour smell
Of sap rose into the air, loud cries
From the scattered women
Running from tree to tree
Vied with the chainsaw roar, and seemed to madden

Their enemy into a state
Of apoplectic outrage . . . Up ahead
He saw a great blossoming tree, a dogwood
Held by some to house the wood's own spirit;
Gashing it with his blade
He sprang back in surprise:
Out of the wound poured sap the colour of blood:

A scarlet banner unfurling
Into the *White and Blue* . . . and then the tall
Glittering dome of the tree began to fall;
Twisting, the leaves and blossom swirling,
Trunk splintering like a bone,
And as it crashed, the whole
Wood and hillside echoed with the groan.

3

Meanwhile Gendenwitha came
To the waterfall, where on her knees
She prayed out loud: 'Demeter, Ishtar, Ceres,
Papothkwe (to use my people's name)—
Life force of every plant;

You whose reality
We've honoured to this day in blind faith, grant

Some token of yourself, and if
Our love can't bring you into being
Then let this man's brutality.' So saying,
She looked up at the foam-curtained cliff
And in the rainbow glaze
Saw suddenly the bright
Voluptuous shimmering figure of the goddess.

Trembling, dazzled, she heard a voice
Close in her ear like a rush of wind
Whisper: 'Daughter, follow this stream till you find
A cinderblock shack. This is the House
Of Hunger. Go inside,
Tell Hunger to visit
Erisychthon.' With which the vision faded.

So the woman set out along
The twisting stream that led through the wood
Where its pure waters took on a tint of blood
From the sacred tree. From there the long
Fall past fields and quarries,
Cities, suburbs, thruways,
Stockyards and junkyards, strip-mines, foundries, factories

Added a number of other
Interesting tints to the stream—spilt oil,
Solvents, pesticides, slurries, lead—until
Nothing was left for Gendenwitha
To follow but a thin
Ooze of mud-coloured sludge
That crawled across a desolate moonlike plain

Of exhausted farmland; barren,
Skeletal orchards, rusting silos,

Dry irrigation pipes crisscrossing meadows
Of dust, with here and there a warren
Of crooked-chimneyed huts,
Slumped trailers where old cars
Sank in the mud out front, and starving mutts

Skulked by trashcans; till at last
A little cinderblock shack appeared:
Doorless, derelict-looking . . . The woman peered
Into the shadows. There in the dust
Sat a hollow-eyed child
Dressed in rags, neglected;
Over her wizened, listless face hung soiled

Clumps of thin hair; her lips were cracked,
Sores crusted her throat, her brittle bones
Stuck out under her scooped-out shoulders and loins,
And long claws seemed to have gouged the racked
Furrows in her ribcage.
This was Hunger. A spoon
Dangled from her hand, and a look of reproach,

Ancient and unappeasable,
Glistened in her eyes. Without a word
She listened to Ceres' commands and followed
The woman back up the stream until
They reached the road that led
To Erisychthon's house.
Night had fallen. The great man lay in bed

Snoring too loud to hear his door
Creak open and Hunger slip inside.
Climbing onto the bed, she squatted astride
His chest, then down through his gaping jaw
Inserted her long spoon
And in one deft movement
Emptied him out, then pressed his lips with her own,

Breathing herself into his blood
Till famine blazed there . . . Then out she crept
Back to her hovel. As Erisychthon slept
He started dreaming vividly of food:
Hunks of succulent meat,
In pungent sauces; pies,
Pastries, ripe cheeses; raising a forkful to eat,

He ground his teeth on air, and woke
With a strange fierce hunger in his guts . . .
Down at the fridge he rummaged for cold cuts,
Then called his daughter and had her cook
A breakfast of waffles,
Homefries, bacon and eggs,
And wolfed it down. Within an hour or less

He was hungry again, and called
For another breakfast—'And this time
Don't skimp on me. Let's see, we'll start with a prime
Rib of Black Angus, then a nice grilled
Turkey and Swiss on rye,
Then I think apple cake
With maple whipped cream . . . No, make that pecan pie,

'Or both in fact.' The girl obeyed.
He gulped down the meal, went off to work
Up at Cascade with his men, where hunger struck
Once again with a pang that made
His flesh pour sweat like wax
From a melting candle:
So about-turn, stopping off for Big Macs

And cheese-steaks . . . Back at home he ordered
His dumbstruck daughter to cook him up
'Something substantial. None of this diet crap.
Give me some corned beef hash, some breaded
Pork chops. I want meat loaf,

Donuts and marshmallows,
Bake me some shrimp . . . Don't stand there gaping. Move!'

So it continued, day and night;
Daughter cooking while her father ate,
Breaking off only to breathe and defecate,
Then only to breathe: his appetite
Was such that he was soon
Obliged to take his meals
(Or rather his one endless meal) on the throne,

Where like an upturned alchemist,
He steadily turned his gold to shit:
Cash, vintage cars, then the yacht, then bit by bit
The land, the house itself, till the last
Dollar slid down the drain
And he and his daughter
Found themselves abruptly out in the rain

Without a penny. What to do?
Beg on street corners? The nickels fell
Like a few useless waterdrops in hell
On the flames of his appetite, which grew
Livelier and hotter
Every minute till sheer
Pain brought inspiration: 'I'll sell my daughter!'

So for ten bucks he pimped the child
There on the street (this touching detail
Is taken straight from Ovid's original,
Just in case the reader thinks we've piled
It on a bit too thick);
But while the girl was gone
A sudden pang of hunger like a mule-kick

Stabbed his belly . . . He had to eat
Something, anything, without delay:

Smashing a butcher's window, he grabbed a tray
Of sirloin slabs and fled down the street
Tearing off lumps of steak
With his teeth as he ran
Up out of town to the woods, where like a shark

In a feeding frenzy, he lost
All distinction between what was food
And what was his living flesh: with a jagged
Blade of slate he hacked a plump red roast
From his own arm; the bone
Soon glistened white, stripped bare;
And just as he'd mauled the trees, he mauled his own

Limbs and trunk in a consuming
Fury of hunger and pain until
He'd eaten half his body. A certain pool,
Mentioned before, lay quietly fuming
In the damp air close by:
Here, as Erisychthon
Staggered onward, reeling from tree to tree

Deranged, blood-spattered like a bear
Savaged by wolves—himself both victim
And pack of predators tearing at each limb—
He paused, and lapped the potent water,
Then limped off upward, drawn
By a stumbling instinct
Back to the scene of his desecration.

A sewage ditch now crossed the bulldozed
Building site: he tumbled in, and here
His mutilated shape began to alter
Into its own double-orificed
Essence of greed and waste;
Mouth and rear end opening
To two huge O's; stomach and barrel chest

Hollowing out from rim to rim,
Hardening as his limbs disappeared
And nothing was left of him but a yard
Of concrete pipe. And there we leave him,
Soon to be delivered
From his own emptiness
Forever, or at least until the wood

Reclaims Cascade.
                  Meanwhile beyond,
Much remains still to be spoiled: in fall
Hillsides still assemble their unsaleable
Red and yellow mosaics; on every pond
Floats the same old mottled
Surrealist carpet; green
Globes of foliage dip themselves in gold

For no discernible purpose.
Then come dustier colours; ochres,
Tawny oranges, browns of bracts and burrs,
Bristly asters, leafless trees like patches
Of worn plush in a once
Sumptuous court's faded
Velvet upholstery, where skeletons

Gemmed with crab-apples breathe a sour
Musk of cider . . . Then winter arrives:
Pathos of moulting angels, arthritic leaves
Gloved by hissing snow that in an hour
Fashions a scrupulous
Translation of each tree
Into a bright new language, and then blows

Its work to pieces, as doubtless
Every translator should. Then springtime's
Mint of glinting coinage—a billion dimes—
Tumbles out of dry twigs; superfluous

Miracle we cherish
Each year more anxiously
As if the very notion of a fresh

Beginning has begun to fray
And seem implausible; as if
Against life's optimistic faith in life
Too much evidence has come to weigh,
And almost everything
It liked about itself
Suddenly seems autumnal, even spring.

Hercules, Deianira, Nessus

C. K. WILLIAMS

There was absolutely no reason after the centaur had pawed her and tried
      to mount her,
after Hercules waiting across the raging river for the creature to carry her
      to him
heard her cry out and launched an arrow soaked in the Hydra's incurable
      venom into the monster,
that Deianira should have believed him, Nessus, horrible thing, as he
      died, but she did.

We see the end of the story: Deianira anguished, aghast, suicide-sword
      in her hand;
Hercules's blood hissing and seething like water into which molten rods
      are plunged to anneal,
but how could a just-married girl hardly out of her father's house have
      envisioned all that,
and even conjecturing that Nessus was lying, plotting revenge, how could
      she have been sure?

We see the centaur as cunning, malignant, a hybrid from the savage time
      before ours
when emotion always was passion and passion was always unchecked by
      commandment or conscience;
she sees only a man-horse, mortally hurt, suddenly harmless, eyes sud-
      denly soft as a foal's,
telling her, 'Don't be afraid, come closer, listen': offering homage, friend-
      ship, a favor.

In our age of scrutiny and dissection we know Deianira's mind better
      than she does herself:
we know the fortune of women as chattel and quarry, objects to be won
      then shunted aside;

we understand the cost of repression, the repercussions of unsatisfied rage
     and resentment,
but consciousness then was still new, Deianira inhabited hers like the
     light from a fire.

Or might she have glimpsed with that mantic prescience the gods hadn't
     taken away yet
her hero a lifetime later on the way home with another king's daughter,
     callow, but lovely,
lovely enough to erase from Hercules's scruples not only his vows but the
     simple convention
that tells you you don't bring a rival into your aging wife's weary, sorrowful
     bed?

. . . No, more likely the centaur's promise intrigued in itself: an infallible
     potion of love.
'Just gather the clots of blood from my wound: here, use my shirt, then
     hide it away.
Though so exalted, so regal a woman as you never would need it, it might
     still be of use:
whoever's shoulders it touches, no matter when, will helplessly, hopelessly
     love you forever.'

See Hercules now, in the shirt Deianira has sent him, approaching the
     fire of an altar,
the garment suddenly clinging, the Hydra, his long-vanquished foe, alive
     in its threads,
each thread a tentacle clutching at him, each chemical tentacle acid,
     adhering, consuming,
charring before his horrified eyes skin from muscle, muscle from tendon,
     tendon from bone.

Now Deianira, back then, the viscous gouts of Nessus's blood dyeing her
     diffident hands:
if she could imagine us watching her there in her myth, how would she
     want us to see her?
Surely as symbol, a petal of sympathy caught in the perilous rift between
     culture and chaos,

not as the nightmare she is, a corpse with a slash of tardy self-knowledge
    deep in its side.

What Hercules sees as he pounds up the bank isn't himself cremated
    alive on his pyre,
shrieking as Jove his Olympian father extracts his immortal essence from
    its agonized sheath:
he sees what's before him: the woman, his bride, kneeling to the dark,
    rushing river,
obsessively scrubbing away, he must think, the nocuous, mingled reek of
    horse, Hydra, human.

A Ballad of Iole and Dryope

CHARLES TOMLINSON

As we walked by the water, my sister and I,
We were plucking the flowers that grew in the way,
As fresh as the spring and the child that she fed
Whose wandering eyes their colours delighted.
A tree rose before us, close to the shore:
A lotus it seemed from the blossoms it bore,
And her hand was already stretched out to the stem
And snapping off stalks as she gathered them.
What I saw, and she did not, was blood from each wound
Drop from the blossoms and sully the ground,
And a tremor passed through that shook the whole tree
(So the tale may be true that taught us to see
Lotis the nymph flee Priapus's flame
And change to this plant that still carries her name).
Astonished, Dryope drew back from the blood,
Yet paused there to plead with the nymphs of the flood,
'Forgive my unknowing and cleanse me of sin',
Half-turned with her child, and yet could not begin
To break from the spot and to run to the wood:
Already her limbs, taking root where she stood,
Had started the changes that she must pass through
As she felt the encroachment of bark from below
Spread stealthily upwards, possess without haste
The freedom to move in her loins and her waist,
Until the sole motion her body still knows
Comes from above, but comes to confuse:
Trembling, her hands reach up to her hair—
Leaves rustle against her fingertips there.
In the mind of the child that was still at her breast
Came a sense of the hardness against which it pressed,
And loss of that moisture its mouth vainly sought
Brought a new lack into wakening thought.

We'd come here with garlands, and all for the sake
Of the powers that rule in the depths of the lake,
But fate has undone us and darkened their mood:
They lurk underwater in silent ingratitude.
What could I do, merely destined to see
The bole that was body transformed to a tree,
To rescue Dryope and set her limbs free?
I tried by embracing to hold back the growth
And longed for the bark to envelop us both.
Her husband and father, aroused by her cries,
Emerged to behold how her branches arise;
They printed their kisses against the harsh rind,
Embracing her roots as they knelt on the ground,
Repeated her name, as if that might still free
The woman not yet disappeared in the tree:
Until it was only her face that now kept
A human resemblance where bark had not crept.
With tears now bedewing the leaves she had grown
She struggled to speak before all words were gone.
'Before I am changed into merely a thing,
Let my innocence tell how my sufferings spring
From the gods' own indifference, not from my deed,
For my will was asleep in what my hands did.
If this be untrue, let all my leaves fade
And axes cut back all my boughs and their shade,
And fire crackle through the ruin they've made.
But take down my son from these branches my arms
And find him a nurse to soothe the child's qualms;
Let him often be brought where these branches are spread
And here let him play and here let him be fed.
Teach him, when words are beginning, to say
"It is my own mother lies lost in this tree."
Let him master my name and pronounce it with tears,
Let him, when later in woods he appears,
Beware of the pools there and think that he sees
A goddess concealed in each one of the trees
And spare every blossom that grows from the bough.
Husband, sister and father, adieu to you now,

But if in your hearts there is love for me still,
Secure me from cattle, protect my boughs well
Against billhook and blade. Take my final adieu,
And since my stiff form cannot bend to kiss you,
Reach up to my lips and lift me my son,
To receive my last kiss, while kiss I still can.
But the bark as it spreads is sealing my lips,
And over my lily-white neck the rind creeps.
My head lost in shades, let none touch my eyes—
To close them the bark of itself will suffice.'
Then both speech and being the same moment cease.
On the trunk the glow of the human still warmed,
And so ends The Tale of Dryope Transformed.

Iphis and Ianthe

FLEUR ADCOCK

But that's nothing to what happened in Crete.
Once upon a time there was a man
called Ligdus, from near Knossos—a nobody,
but freeborn, honourable and decent.
His wife was pregnant. When her time was close,
this is what he told her: 'I pray for two things:
a painless labour for you, and a son.
Girls are more trouble, and I can't afford one.
So—God forgive me—if by some awful chance
the baby's female, she will have to be killed.'
Then both burst into tears, and Telethusa
pleaded with her husband, but he was adamant.

When her heavy womb could scarcely hold
its load, at midnight she had a vision:
she saw, or thought she saw, the goddess Isis
standing by her bed in royal splendour,
crowned with crescent horns and wheat-ears of gold
and attended by dog-headed Anubis,
the bull-god Apis, the cat Bubastis,
and the god of silence, his finger to his lips.
'Stop grieving, Telethusa,' Isis said.
'Ignore your husband; keep whatever child
may come. You've been my loyal worshipper.
I'm not ungrateful, and you'll find me helpful.'

So when the baby, of its own accord,
pushed its way out and proved to be a girl,
its mother told the nurse (her only partner
in the fraud): 'Take care of my little boy.'
They got away with it—Ligdus never guessed.
He called the child after its grandfather:

Iphis, a gender-free name (which pleased
Telethusa—no need for deception there).
Somehow the trick—an honourable one,
since the gods approved—fooled everyone. The child
was dressed as a boy, and had the kind of looks
that would have done credit to either sex.

Years passed, and when Iphis was thirteen
her father arranged for his daughter to be married
to another girl, golden-haired Ianthe,
a famous beauty. They were school-mates, these two,
equal in age, equally good-looking,
and equally in love with one another;
far from equal, though, in their expectations:
Ianthe was looking forward to her marriage,
assuming that the person who was to be
her husband would turn out to be a man.
Iphis loved someone she despaired of enjoying—
a fact which only served to fan the flames.

This is what she said, almost in tears:
'What future is there for me—for a woman
in love with a woman, a freakish and unheard-of
passion? Cows don't fall in love with cows,
or mares with mares. A ewe fancies a ram,
a doe runs after a stag. Even birds do it
normally, like the whole animal kingdom.
If only I weren't female! True, Pasiphaë
loved a bull; but at least it was male.
She had her way with it, disguised as a heifer;
but not Daedalus himself, if he flew back
on his wax wings, could magic me a sex-change.

'Come on, then, Iphis, pull yourself together.
Shake off this useless doting. Be what you are,
and love what women are permitted to love.
It's hope that breeds love, hope that feeds it,
but the facts deny you hope. No jealous husband

or cruel father keeps you from her arms,
nor the girl herself. The obstacle is nature,
that force more powerful than any . . . But look:
the day's at hand. Ianthe will be mine—
and not mine. I shall be thirsty amid water.
Why should Juno and Hymen come to a wedding
where there's no bridegroom, and both of us are brides?'

Meanwhile Ianthe longed for the ceremony—
while Telethusa did her best to postpone it,
inventing illnesses, dreams, bad omens.
But when all her excuses had run out
and the day was imminent, she unbound her hair
and her daughter's and, all dishevelled, prayed:
'Isis, goddess, you who dwell in the lands
of Egypt, by the Nile with its seven horns,
help us! I saw you once, with all your symbols
and your retinue; I listened to your commands.
My daughter was kept alive by your orders.
Have pity on us both, and come to our aid!'

She wept. And then it seemed to her that the goddess
moved her altars—yes, and the temple doors
were shaking, the crescent horns flashed with light . . .
Uncertain still but excited, Telethusa
left the temple. Iphis walked by her side—
with a longer stride than usual; her fair skin
lost its pallor; she seemed to have gained in strength;
her features were more rugged, her hair shorter.
She was a boy! Now for fearless rejoicing
and thank-offerings. They wrote this verse on a plaque:
  The gifts which as a girl he made a vow
  to bring, the young man Iphis presents now.

Next morning, daylight streamed across the world
when Venus, Juno and Hymen all assembled
at the wedding-fires; and Iphis gained his Ianthe.

Orpheus and Eurydice

SEAMUS HEANEY

x, 1–85

Orpheus called for Hymen and Hymen came
Robed in saffron like a saffron flame
Leaping across tremendous airy zones
To reach the land of the Ciconians.
So Hymen did attend the rites, but no
Good luck or cheer or salutations, no
Auspicious outcome was to come of that.
Instead, the torch he carried smoked and spat
And no matter how he fanned it wouldn't flare.
His eyes kept watering. And a worse disaster
Than could have been predicted came to pass
For as the bride went roaming through the grass
With all her naiads round her, she fell down.
A snake had bit her ankle. She was gone.

Orpheus mourned her in the world above,
Lamenting and astray, until his love
Compelled him down among the very shades.
He dared to venture on the Stygian roads
Among those shadow people, the many, many
Ghosts of the buried, to find Persephone
And the lord who rules the dismal land of Hades;
Then tuned the lyre-gut to its own sweetness
And sang in harmony: 'O founded powers
Who rule the underearth, this life of ours,
This mortal life we live in upper air
Will be returned to you. To you, therefore,
We may speak the whole truth and speak it out
As I do now, directly: I have not
Transgressed your gloomy borders just to see

The sights of Tartarus, nor to tie all three
Of the three-necked monster's snake-snarled necks in one.
I crossed into your jurisdiction
Because my wife is here. The snake she stepped on
Poisoned her and cut her off too soon
And though I have tried to suffer on my own
And outlive loss, in the end Love won.
Whether or not you underpowers feel
The force of this god, Love, I cannot tell,
But surely he prevails down here as well
Unless that ancient story about hell
And its lord and a ravaged girl's not true.
Was it not Love that bound the two of you?
I pray you, therefore, by the extent of these
Dark hazy voids and scaresome silences
Unweave the woven fate Eurydice
Endured too soon. All of humanity
Is in your power, your kingdom is our home.
We may put off the day but it will come.
Sooner or later, the last house on the road
Will be this immemorial abode.
This is the throne-room of the universe.
Allow Eurydice her unlived years
And when she will have lived them, she'll be yours
Inalienably. I desire on sufferance
And want my wife. But if the fates pronounce
Against this privilege, then you can take
Credit for two deaths. I shall not go back.'

As Orpheus played and pleaded, the bodiless
Hordes of the dead wept for him. Tantalus
Was so bewitched he let the next wave fill
And fall without reaching. Ixion's wheel
Stood spellbound. The vultures' beaks held off
Above Tityos's liver. The obsessive
Water-riddlers heard and did not move.
And Sisyphus, you dozed upon your rock
Which stood dazed also. A tear then wet the cheek

Of each of the Eumenides, the one
And only time: song had made them human
And made the lord of Hades and his lady
Relent as well. They called Eurydice
Who limped out from among the newly dead
To Orpheus, all eager and transported
And restored. But there was one term set:
Until he left Avernus, he was not
To look back, or the gift would be in vain.

They took the pathway up a steep incline
That kept on rising higher, through a grim
Silence and thick mist, and they had come
Close to the rim of earth when Orpheus—
Anxious for her, wild to see her face—
Turned his head to look and she was gone
Immediately, forever, back and down.
He reached his arms out, desperate to hold
And be held on to, but his arms just filled
With insubstantial air. She died again,
Bridal and doomed, but still did not complain
Against her husband—as indeed how could she
Complain about being loved so totally?
Instead, as she slipped away, she called out dear
And desperate farewells he strained to hear.

The second death stunned Orpheus. He stood
Disconsolate, beyond himself, dumbfounded
Like the man who turned to stone because he'd seen
Hercules lead Cerberus on a chain
Leashed to his middle neck; or like that pair
Petrified to two rocks underwater
In the riverlands of Ida—Olenus
And Lethaea, uxorious sinners.
Pleading and pleading to be let across
The Styx again, he sat for seven days
Fasting and filthy on the bank, but Charon
Would not allow it. So he travelled on

Accusing the cruel gods until he found
A way back to his mountainous home ground
In Rhodope.

       The sun passed through the house
Of Pisces three times then, and Orpheus
Withdrew and turned away from loving women—
Perhaps because there only could be one
Eurydice, or because the shock of loss
Had changed his very nature. Nonetheless,
Many women loved him and, denied
Or not, adored. But now the only bride
For Orpheus was going to be a boy
And Thracians learned from him, who still enjoy
Plucking those spring flowers bright and early.

Death of Orpheus

SEAMUS HEANEY

XI, 1–84

The songs of Orpheus held the woods entranced.
The animals were hushed, the field-stones danced
Until a band of crazed Ciconian women,
A maenad band dressed up in wild beasts' skins,
Spied him from a hilltop with his lyre.
As he tuned his voice to it and cocked his ear,
One of them whose hair streamed in the breeze
Began to shout, 'Look, look, it's Orpheus,
Orpheus the misogynist,' and flung
Her staff straight at the bard's mouth while he sang.
But the staff being twined with leaves just left a bruise
And did no injury. So another throws
A stone that his singing spellbinds in the air,
Making it drop like a shamed petitioner
At his affronted feet. But even so,
There could be no stop to the violence now.
The furies were unleashed. And his magic note
That should have stalled their weapons was drowned out
By blaring horns and drums, beatings and yells
And the pandemonium of those bacchanals
So that at last his red blood wet the rocks.
But first the maenads ripped apart the snakes
And the flocks of birds he'd charmed out of the sky
And the dreambound beasts that formed his retinue.
Orpheus then, torn by their blood-filled nails,
Was like an owl in daytime when it falls
Prey to the hawks of light; or a stag that stands
In the amphitheatre early, before the hounds
Have savaged it to pieces on the sand.

They circled him, still using as their weapons
Staffs they had twined with leaves and tipped with cones
That were never meant for duty such as this.
Some pelted him with clods, some stripped the branches
To scourge him raw, some stoned him with flintstones.
But as their frenzy peaked, they chanced upon
Far deadlier implements.

　　　　　　Near at hand
Oxen in yokes pulled ploughshares through the ground
And sturdy farmers sweated as they dug—
Only to flee across their drills and rigs
When they saw the horde advancing. They downed tools
So there for the taking on the empty fields
Lay hoes and heavy mattocks and long spades.
The oxen lowered their horns, the squealing maenads
Cut them to pieces, then turned to rend the bard,
Committing sacrilege when they ignored
His hands stretched out to plead and the extreme
Pitch of his song that now for the first time
Failed to enchant. And so, alas, the breath
Of life streamed out of him, out of that mouth
Whose songs had tamed the beasts and made stones dance,
And was blown away on the indiscriminate winds.

For Orpheus then the birds in cheeping flocks,
The animals in packs, the flint-veined rocks
And woods that had listened, straining every leaf,
Wept and kept weeping. For it seemed as if
The trees were mourners tearing at their hair
As the leaves streamed off them and the branch went bare.
And rivers too, they say, rose up in floods
Of their own tears, and all the nymphs and naiads
Went dishevelled in drab mourning gowns.
Meanwhile, the poet's mangled flesh and bones
Lay scattered and exposed. But his head and lyre
Were saved by miracle: the Hebrus River
Rose for them, ran with them, bore them out midstream

Where the lyre trembled and the dead mouth swam
Lapping the ripples that lipped the muddy shore
And a fluent humming sadness filled the air.
As they rode the current downstream, they were swept
On out to sea off Lesbos and washed up
On the strand there, unprotected. Then a snake
Unleashed itself like a slick whip to attack
The head in its tangled web of sopping locks
But Phoebus intervened. Just as its bite
Gaped at its widest, it solidified.
The jaws' hinge hardened and the open yawn
Of the empty vicious mouth was set in stone.

The poet's shade fled underneath the earth
Past landmarks that he recognized, down paths
He'd travelled on the first time, desperately
Scouring the blessed fields for Eurydice.
And when he found her, wound her in his arms
And moved with her, and she with him, two forms
Of the one love, restored and mutual—
For Orpheus now walks free, is free to fall
Out of step, into step, follow, go in front
And look behind him to his heart's content.

But Bacchus was unwilling to forget
The atrocities against his sacred poet,
So, there and then, in a web of roots, he wound
And bound the offending women to the ground.
However deftly they would try to go,
Earth's grip and traction clutched them from below.
They felt it latch them, load them heel and toe.
And, as a caught bird struggles to get free
From a cunningly set snare, but still can only
Tighten the mesh around its feet still tighter
The more it strains its wings and frets and flutters,
So each of the landlogged women heaved and hauled
In vain, in agony, as the roots took hold
And bark began to thicken the smooth skin.

It gripped them and crept up above their knees.
They struggled like a storm in storm-tossed trees.
Then, as each finger twigged and toe dug in,
Arms turned to oak boughs, thighs to oak, oak leaves
Matted their breasts and camouflaged their moves
So that you couldn't tell if the whole strange growth
Were a wood or women in distress or both.

Orpheus Dies, and the God Seeks Out Silenus

PETER REDGROVE

i.m. H.S.

It is sweet and decorous
To light the fire in the hearth and dream
Of the death of poets. The boulders
Follow him, scoring huge trenches
To where he sits on a hill, letting the wind
Play his lyre; it was Aeolus who played it
And Orpheus fitted words to the improvised music,
As I do now, to the jumping figures in the fire
That rends and heals, my spliff
Balsamic among the books
Which wear their animal skins, calves
That have followed the music of the books
To my pungent study.

She made the mistake of not stripping
Her spear of its foliage; still,
It marked his lip. Then the women
Brought out their Brenton Drum
And their squeeze-boxes so that nobody
Could hear the words of his last song, and soon
The pursuing stones got their drink of blood.
The birds flew off, having memorized from him
Their versions of song. The ground rippled
With snakes learning to sing. The lions assembled
In the music school, but they feared the women,
The women who ripped the oxen to get the bone-harrows
To reduce the poet. Decorous it is to read
From between the skins of calves

The stories of the deaths of poets.
My roach crackles in my hand.

This is where they left his face
Hanging in this bush; now the world
Will look at us with his face always; this line
Of hedge, this singing tree, this furrowed
Rock, they join to make a landscape-face
Out of the side of the mountain, improvised.

They threw the pieces into the water,
The river took them, the lyre continued
Its extemporization in the flowing water,
The meaty head tried out a note without lungs,
The river rushing through his gory neck
Invented waterspeech. I saw the head washed up and there
Was a snake stretching its jaws ready to devour it,
But somebody turned that snake to stone; I have
That hearthstone still; see how the firelight
Wriggles it. His head still gongs like fire, his
Electrical shade weds Eurydice's earth-electricity;
The mine galleries are charged with it, become
The corridors of their palace which
Improvises music on their draughty corners;
Look into my smoke, see there
The rout of women snatching birds out of the air,
Trampling their songs as the snakes in one enormous
Undulation leave; the boulders heave themselves
Down on the poet.

It was the songs of the spirit of drink
That the Bard extemporized, I say, drawing on my smoke,
It was a drunken misunderstanding. His first drink
Rested in him, and spoke, and that's where
Today's songs came from, he was accustomed
To tipple to get his solo songs, pure poetry
Clear as gin; that was an intolerable
Breach of security of Bacchus' mysteries; the drink

Had not by then destroyed his body,
In fact he looked good until that moment
The good women harrowed him.
They had drunk enough to kill him,
And he had drunk enough to be killed.
I could see the large images of blood
Soaking into the sand, and the rosy
Billows of the river, and I saw the large print
Of his countenance unrolling over the landscape
So that he glanced at me across the river
With that wood, but where had the women gone?

I noticed a fresh grove of young oaks
Arranged in a dancing-pattern; I entered and saw
That the trees creaked wooden speech; having made
That formulation, I detected an unconsumed eyelid
Beating like a butterfly on a branch, fluttering
As the breeze moved into the coppice
And gave it improvisatory speech; I could hear
One of the wood-voices asking
Where her fingers had gone, and another
Crying for her hair: 'Mommy feels like shit!'
'A serious wipeout . . .' 'A mega-hangover!';
The reddened mump in a fold of the rosy river.
Striking her thighs with grief, she struck oak.

Now the Bard drinks the whole river
And they drink the showers from their leaves:
'flebile nescio quid queriter lyra, flebile lingua
murmurat exanimis, respondent flebile ripae'—
And they quaff the subterranean waters through
Their gigantic roots, still growing downwards;

And the god says: 'I have promoted you women
To serious drinking, take it if you will
As punishment by the Bard; or promotion,
As you please; meanwhile I will look
For another Druid, and find out

By trial whether any are serious enough
About drinking to risk transformation,'
Says Bacchus, glad to see his companion Silenus,
For they had beauty between them once, and only
The god was able to keep it; Silenus, as he aged,
Drowned in himself, wallowed
In the sea he had drunk, his own personal sea
Cum shipwreck, his own skiff
Entangled with vines and gradually sinking
Under the weight of the clustering grapes; the god saw
How he erased into a hulk, into a voluble
Reminiscence of all the inns hereabouts, could
Reiterate every jest and cup of wine like a library
Of pottery books, of alcohol
Bound in human skin, that would be wiped when
His brain burst at last; meanwhile he leaked
Through his ever-open penis a subsidiary wine
The fauns tasted and rejoiced in. Or so I calculate,
Sucking on my end of the godlike weed.

Apollo and Hyacinthus

J. D. MCCLATCHY

Guilt's dirty hands, memory's kitchen sink . . .
    It's bad faith makes immortal love.
        Take a closer look at Hyacinth.

Dark bud-tight curls and poppy-seed stubble,
    The skin over his cheekbones pale as poison
        Slowly dripped from eye to eye,

And a crotch that whispers its single secret
    Even from behind the waiter's apron.
        He's pouting now, staring at the traffic.

Every year there's a new one at the bar
    Sprung from whatever nowhere—the country,
        The islands, the middle west . . .

The old man at the far corner table, decades ago
    Called by his critics 'the sun god
        Of our poetry', sits stirring

A third coffee and an opening line,
    Something like *So often you renew*
        Yourself or *You and I resemble*

Every other pair of lovers.
    The grease stain on his left sleeve
        Winks as the lights come on.

He signals the boy and means to ask
    Under cover of settling the check
        If, with the usual understanding

And for the same pleasures, he'd return again
    Tonight, after work, there was something
        He'd wanted to show the boy, a picture

Of two sailors that if held upside down . . .
    It's then he notices the gold cufflinks
        The boy is wearing, the pair the poet's

Friends had given him when his first book—
    That moist sheaf of stifled longings—
        Appeared in Alexandria.

To have stolen from one who would give
    Anything: what better pretext
        To put the end to 'an arrangement'?

The old man falls silent, gets up from his seat,
    Leaves a few coins on the table
        And walks out through his confusions,

Homeward through the sidestreets, across the square,
    Up the fifty-two stone steps, up the years
        And back to his study, its iron cot.

The heaving had stopped. The last sad strokes
    Of the town clock had rung: Anger was one,
        Humiliation the other.

He sat there until dawn and wrote out the poem
    That has come to be in all the anthologies,
        The one you know, beginning

You are my sorrow and my fault. The one that goes
    In all my songs, in my mind, in my mouth,
        The sighing still sounds of you.

The one that ends with the boy—the common,
　　Adored, two-timing hustler—turned
　　　　Into a flower, *the soft-fleshed lily*

But of a bruised purple that grief will come
　　To scar with its initials AI, AI.
　　　　O, the ache insists.

Pygmalion and Galatea

DEREK MAHON

. . . Pygmalion watched these women, hard-
featured and cynical, as they led
their shameful lives and, sickened by
the wickedness so generously
given to their sex, he lived alone
without a wife to call his own.
Meanwhile, ingeniously, he wrought
a maiden out of ivory, one
lovelier than any woman born,
and with this shape he fell in love.
Alive, she seemed, and apt to move
if modesty did not prevent—
so did his art conceal his art.
He gazed at her in wonderment
and felt her limbs to be quite sure
that she was bone and nothing more.
Her skin responded to his stroke,
or so he thought; and so he spoke,
seized her, imagining his thick
fingers sank into her back,
and looked for bruises on the work.
He whispered gentle, loving words,
brought presents, shells and pebbles, birds
and flowers, things that please young girls;
he clothed her, putting diamond rings
on her white fingers, ropes of pearls
about her neck and breasts. These things
were gorgeous, certainly, although
the naked sculpture even more so
He laid her down on a bed spread
with sheets dyed a Tyrian red,
called her his lover, propped her head

among soft, feathery pillows as if
a statue might have sensuous life.
   Now Venus' feast-day was the date
and Cyprus thronged to celebrate.
Heifers, their spread horns freshly gilt,
had felt the death-stroke to the hilt
in their soft necks, as white as snow,
and the air smoked with incense. Now
Pygmalion, having devoutly laid
gifts on the altar, shyly prayed:
'Gods, if it's true that you can give
anything, grant I may make love—'
Too shy to say 'the maid', he said,
'—to someone *like* my ivory maid!'
But Venus, there in person, knew
what he intended and, to show
that she approved, the altar flames
shot up into the air three times.
Hastening home, the impatient lover
ran to the maid and, leaning over,
embraced her there on her chaste couch.
Her skin seemed warmer to his touch;
his fingers felt her thighs, at which
the ivory grew soft between
his thumbs, as wax melts in the sun
and, gently worked by loving hands,
stretches, relaxes and expands,
responsive even as it responds.
   He stood amazed, still doubtful, thought
himself mistaken, and then not;
inflamed, he stroked her thighs again
until the statue moved! Each vein
fluttered as our protagonist,
pouring out thanks to Venus, thrust
his lips upon live lips at last.
The maid, feeling his kisses, raised
shy eyes to the sun and, at a glance,

saw daylight and his face at once.
The goddess, with her genial presence,
sanctioned the union and in time
a girl, Paphos, was born to them—
from whom the island takes its name.

Ivory and Water

MICHAEL LONGLEY

If as a lonely bachelor who disapproves of women
You carve the perfect specimen out of snow-white ivory
And fall in love with your masterpiece and make love to her
(Or try to), stroking, fondling, whispering, kissing, nervous
In case you bruise ivory like flesh with prodding fingers,
And bring sea-shells, shiny pebbles, song-birds, colourful wild
Flowers, amber beads, orchids, beach-balls as her presents,
And put real women's clothes, wedding rings, ear-rings, long
Necklaces, a brassière on the statue, then undress her
And lay her in your bed, her head on the feathery pillows
As if to sleep like a girlfriend, your dream may come true
And she warms and softens and you are kissing actual lips
And she blushes as she takes you in, the light of her eyes,
And her veins pulse under your thumb to the end of the dream
When she breaks out in a cold sweat that trickles into pools
And drips from her hair dissolving it and her fingers and toes,
Watering down her wrists, shoulders, rib-cage, breasts until
There is nothing left of her for anyone to hug or hold.

Myrrha

FREDERICK SEIDEL

A daughter loved her father so much
She accused him of sexual abuse.
But I am getting ahead of my story.
Ten years after
He had simply been being a good father
She made the charge.
But I am ruining it.
Not that the man was ever told.
And when the accused is not even advised
He has been accused,
And is therefore deprived of a chance to defend himself, society—
Shit! the teleprompter stopped—
Which camera is on?
So it goes these days
With the help of radical feminist therapy
Redressing so many obvious wrongs.
Also because the specialists
Advise against confronting the incestuous rapist
Who may of course have done nothing and be innocent,
But who if he has will deny it to the grave.
One slightly feels he must have done something for the charge
In the first place to have been made.

Muse, put your breast in my mouth
If you want me to sing.
(Fuck the muse.)

Sunlight yellow as a canary.
Perfume from the garden made the room tropical.
The maid in her uniform struggles to draw the heavy curtains.
Darkness in spasms spreads as she tugs.

Light covers the hot and humid girl on the bed
And then is yanked away
By the maid. The last light the maid sees slants across
The girl's eyes and nose like a blindfold.
One of the eyes is green as an emerald.
The fourteen-year-old nose is classical.
The eyes are open in the darkness.
Darkness shrink-wraps her
And where her hands are.
The maid leaves the room adjusting herself.

Please,
The girl says to her father, Please
Let me go to Harvard, Daddy.
They are on a cruise.
The water the white ship cuts through is flowers.
The tube they lean their elbows on is warm.
The sky is black. The stars are out.
White birds fly overhead in the middle of the ocean.
Bam bam
Men are shooting skeet on a higher deck.
Her mother is up there shooting.
The girl is in the stateroom with her father
Who is panting as if he were
Having a heart attack while she undresses.
She can't stop herself.
They are doing it.

The maid comes in the room without knocking.
It is time to wake the princess from her nap.
She pulls the curtains back
And finds the girl
Standing naked on a chair.

She has a noose around
Her neck attached to nothing,
Which is a metaphor for love.

If you really love your father that much,
The maid says an hour later
To the naked girl in her arms,
I will have to do something.

It happens that
The girl's mother is off at Canyon Ranch,
Best of the Fat Farms, getting in shape.
She has been there already a week,
And the king is extremely interested when he is told
One of the women in the palace
Is obsessed with His Highness.
Oh, really, how old?
Oh, young, about your daughter's age.

The girl walks into her dream
Late that night when the maid arrives to take her
To her father.
A bird throbbily coos in the warm darkness outside.
The night air smells so sweet.
She immediately trips and knows perfectly well
What that means, but can't, won't, not.
The maid is sexually excited.
The virgin is in a delirium.

It's the familiar fear-of-heights terror
Of being irresistibly drawn
To the edge. You fall
From the other side of the edge toward the street
To get to Mars.
She feels the moisture of desire.

The man is fast asleep after a lot of drinking
So when the maid says, This is the one,
In the dark room he at first grabs the maid,
Who redirects his hands, and he is immediately
Inside the girl.

For the next two nights the maid
Stands outside in the corridor perspiring,
With her eyes tightly shut, clenching and unclenching her fists.

The father has hidden a flashlight next to his penis in the darkness
In the bed so he can see
Who it is the next night,
When it dawns on him he can simply turn the light on.
He does and tries to kill her,
But she is too fast.
The next thing he hears she is in Sagaponack.
She backtracks to Islip and flies
Out west and keeps going to Hawaii and Bali and on.
She sees the Komodo dragons twenty feet long
And carnivorous and fast and keeps going.
Sri Lanka, southern India, Myanmar
(Where Ne Win, the senile military dictator who has tried to ruin
Rangoon and everywhere else and everyone, still keeps the daughter
Of the great patriot democrat of the country
Under house arrest, but one day that will end).
For nine months she travels, pregnant.

On the day she turns into a tree,
She gives birth to a boy.

Venus and Adonis

TED HUGHES

A power in the air hears the last prayer
Of the desperate. Myrrh's prayer to be no part
Of either her life or her death was heard and was answered.

The earth gripped both her ankles as she prayed.
Roots pried from beneath her toenails, they burrowed
Among deep stones to the bedrock. She swayed,

Living statuary on a tree's foundations.
In that moment her bones became grained wood,
Their marrow pith,

Her blood sap, her arms boughs, her fingers twigs,
Her skin rough bark. And already
The gnarling crust has coffined her swollen womb.

It swarms over her breasts. It warps upwards
Reaching for her eyes as she bows
Eagerly into it, hurrying the burial

Of her face and her hair under smothering bark.
Now all her feeling has gone into wood, with her body.
Yet she weeps,

The warm drops ooze from her rind.
These tears are still treasured.
To this day they are known by her name—Myrrh.

Meanwhile the meaty fruit her father implanted
Has ripened in the bole. Past its term,
It heaves to rive a way out of its mother.

But Myrrh's cramps are clamped in the heart-wood's vice.
Her gagged convulsions cannot leak a murmur.
She cannot cry to heaven for Lucina.

Nevertheless a mother's agony
Strains in the creaking tree and her tears drench it.
For pity, heaven's midwife, Lucina,

Lays her hands on the boughs in their torment
As she recites the necessary magic.
The trunk erupts, the bark splits, and there tumbles

Out into the world with a shattering yell
The baby Adonis. Nymphs of the flowing waters
Cradle him in grasses. They wash him

With his mother's tears. Bittermost envy
Could only glorify such a creature.
A painter's naked Cupid to perfection—

The god's portrait without his arrow quiver,
Or if he had worn one. Here, the subtlest thing,
Too slight for the human eye, time slips past.

And this miraculous baby of his sister,
Sired by his grandpa, just now born of a bush,
Barely a boy, in the blink of an eye is a man

Suddenly more beautiful than ever—
So beautiful the great Venus herself,
Hovering over the wonder, feels awe.

Then the boy's mother, pent by Venus
In that shrub of shame, finds her revenge.
The Goddess falls helplessly for Adonis.

Venus plucking kisses from her Cupid
Snagged her nipple on an unnoticed arrow
Sticking from his quiver. She pushed him away—

But was wounded far worse than she feared.
Pierced with the mortal beauty of Adonis
She has forgotten Cythera's flowery island,

Forgotten the bright beaches of Paphos,
Forgotten Cnidos, delicate as its fish;
Amathus, veined with costly metals. Neglected

Even Olympus. She abstains from heaven
Besotted by the body of Adonis.
Wherever he goes, clinging to him she goes.

She who had loved equally the shade
And her indolence in it, who had laboured
Only as a lily of the valley

Now goes bounding over the stark ridges,
Skirts tucked high like the huntress, or she plunges
Down through brambly goyles, bawling at hounds,

Hunting the harmless: the hare who sees best backwards,
Hinds with painful eyes like ballerinas,
Tall stags on their dignity. She has nothing

To do with fatal boars. She shuns wolves,
Their back teeth always aching to crack big bones.
Bears with a swipe like a dungfork. Lions,

Lank bellies everlastingly empty,
That lob over high bomas, as if weightless,
With bullocks in their jaws. 'These,' she cried,

'O my beloved, are your malefic planets.
Never hesitate to crush a coward
But, challenged by the brave, conceal your courage.

'Leave being bold, my love, to the uglier beasts.
Else you stake my heart in a fool's gamble.
Let Nature's heavier criminals doze on

'Or you may win your glory at my cost.
The beauty, the youth, the charms that humbled Venus
Feel silly and go blank when suddenly a lion

Looks their way. They have no influence
On whatever lifts a boar's bristles,
Or on the interests or on the affections

'Of any of that gang. The tusk of the boar
Is the lightning jag that delivers the bolt.
The ignorant impact of solidified

Hunger in the arrival of a lion
Turns everything to dust. I abhor them!'

'But why should you abhor them?'
'There is a lesson

'These coarse brutes can teach us. But first,
This hunter's toil is more than my limbs are used to.
Look, that kindly poplar has made cool

'A bed of shade in the grass, just for us.'
So Venus pillowed her head on the chest of Adonis.
Then, to her soft accompaniment of kisses:

> 'Once the greatest runner was a woman—so swift
> She outran every man.
> It is true. She could and she did.
> But none could say which was more wonderful—
> The swiftness of her feet or her beauty.

'When this woman questioned the oracle
About her future husband
The god said: "Atalanta,
Stay clear of a husband.
Marriage is not for you. Nevertheless

' "You are fated to marry.
And therefore fated, sooner or later, to live
Yourself but other." The poor girl,
Pondering this riddle, alarmed,
Alerted, alone in a thick wood,

'Stayed unmarried.
The suitors who kept at her stubbornly
She met
With a fearful deterrent:
"You can win me," she told them,

' "Only if you can outrun me.
That is to say, if you will race against me.
Whoever wins that race—he is my husband.
Whoever loses it—has lost his life.
This is the rule for all who dare court me."

'Truly she had no pity.
But the very ferocity
Of this grim condition of hers
Only lent her beauty headier power—
Only made her suitors giddier.

'Hippomenes watched the race.
"What fool," he laughed, "would wager life itself
Simply to win a woman—
With a foregone conclusion against him?
This is a scheme to rid the world of idiots."

'But even as he spoke he saw the face
Of Atalanta. Then as her dress opened

And fell to her feet
He saw her dazzling body suddenly bared.
A beauty, O Adonis, resembling mine

'Or as yours would be if you were a woman.

'Hippomenes' brain seemed to turn over. His arms,
As if grabbing to save himself as he slipped,
Were reaching towards her, fingers hooked,
And he heard his own voice
Coming like somebody else's: "What am I saying?

' "I did not know, I never guessed
What a trophy
You run for—"
And there, as he stammered and stared,
His own heart was lost.

'Suddenly he was terrified of a winner.
He prayed that all would fail and be executed.
"But why," he muttered, "am I not out among them
Taking my chance?
Heaven helps those who give it something to help."

'These words were still whirling in his head
As her legs blurred past him.
Though her velocity was an arrow
As from a Turkish bow of horn and sinew
The shock-wave was her beauty.

'Her running redoubled her beauty.
The ribbon-ties at her ankles
Were the wing-tips of swallows.
The ribbon-ties at her knees
Were the wing-tips of swifts.

'Her hair blazed above her oiled shoulders.
And the flush on her slender body

Was ivory tinted
By rays that glow
Through a crimson curtain.

'And while this hero gazed with drying mouth
It was over.
Atalanta stood adjusting her victor's chaplet
And her defeated suitors, under the knife,
Sprawled as they coughed up her bloody winnings.

'Hippomenes ignored the draining corpses.
He stepped forward—his eyes gripping hers.
"Why do you scry for fame, Atalanta,
In the entrails
Of such pathetic weaklings?

' "Why not run against me?
If I win
You will not be shamed—only surpassed
By the son of Megareus, who was sired by Onchestius,
Who was sired by Neptune, god of the sea.

' "I am Hippomenes—
A great grandson of the god of the oceans.
I have not disappointed expectations.
If my luck fails, by the fame of Hippomenes
Your fame shall be that much more resplendent."

'Atalanta was astonished as she felt
Her heart falter. Her legs began to tremble.
Her wild rage to conquer seemed to have kneeled
In a prayer to be conquered.
She murmured:

' "Which god, jealous of beautiful youth,
Plots now to slay this one?
Putting it into his head to fling away life.

As I am the judge:
Atalanta is not worth it.

' "It is not his beauty that makes me afraid
Though it well might.
It is his innocence, his boyishness
Touches me, and hurts me.
He is hardly a boy. He is a child.

' "Yet with perfect courage,
Contemptuous of death.
Also fourth in descent, as he claims, from the sea-god.
Also, he loves me
And is ready to die if he cannot have me.

' "Listen, stranger.
Get as far away from me as you can
By the shortest route.
Marriage with me is death.
Go while you can move.

' "My bridal bed, my virgin bed, is a sump
Under the executioner's block.
Go and go quickly.
No other woman will refuse you.
The wisest will do all she can to win you.

' "Yet why should I bother myself
After so gladly killing so many?
Why should I care now? Die if you must.
If these poor corpses here cannot deter you,
If you are so sick of your life—then die.

' "They will say: because he dared to love her
She killed him. I shall have to hear:
Her thanks for his fearless love was a shameful death.
This will bring me fame—but ill-fame.
Yet none of it is my fault.

' "You cannot win, Hippomenes.
Forget me.
If only your insanity could shrink
Into your feet as a superhuman swiftness!
Look at him. His face is like a girl's.

' "In me there sleeps evil for both of us.
Do not wake it up. Go quietly away.
You belong to life. But believe me,
If Fate had not made my favour lethal
You alone would be my choice."

'Atalanta knew nothing about love
So she failed
To recognize love's inebriation
As it borrowed her tongue to pronounce these words.
She was hardly aware of what they meant.

'But her father, and the crowd, demanded the race.
And Hippomenes was already praying: "O Venus,
You gave me this great love—now let me keep it."
A quirk of air brought his prayer to my hearing.
Moved, I moved quickly.

'The most precious acre in Cyprus
Is my temple's orchard. A tree grows there
Of solid gold. With leaves of green gold
On boughs of white gold. Among those leaves
Hang apples of red gold. I picked three.

'Visible only to Hippomenes
I taught him the use of these apples.
Then at a blast from the trumpets
Both shot from their marks.
Their feet flickered away and the dust hung.

'They could have been half-flying over water
Just marring the shine.

Or over the silky nape of a field of barley.
Hippomenes felt the crowd's roar lifting him on:
"Hippomenes! You can win! Hippomenes!"

'And maybe Atalanta
Was happier than he was to hear that shout
As she leaned back on her hips, reining back
The terrible bolt of speed in her dainty body,
And clung to him with her glance even as she left him

'Tottering as if to a halt, labouring for air
That scorched his mouth and torched his lungs
With most of the course to go. This was the moment
For flinging one of my apples out past her—
He bounced it in front of her feet and away to the left.

'Startled to see such a gorgeous trinket
Simply tossed aside, she could not resist it.
While she veered to snatch it up
Hippomenes was ahead, breasting the crest
Of the crowd's roar.

'But Atalanta came back in with a vengeance.
She passed him so lightly he felt to be stumbling.
Out went the second apple.
As if this were as easy she swirled and caught it
Out of a cloud of dust and again came past him.

'Now he could see the flutter of the crowd at the finish.
"O Venus," he sobbed, "let me have the whole of your gift!"
Then with all his might he hurled
The last apple
Past and beyond her—into a gulley

'Choked with tumbled rock and thorn. She glimpsed it
Vanishing into a waste

Of obstacles and lost seconds.
With two gold apples heavier at each stride
And the finish so near, she tried to ignore it.

'But I forced her to follow. And the moment she found it
That third apple I made even heavier.
Lugging her three gold prizes far behind
Her race was lost. Atalanta belonged to the winner.
So their story begins.

'But tell me, Adonis, should he have given me thanks
And burned costly perfumes in my honour?
Neither thanks nor perfumes arrived. He forgot my help.

'Anger overtook me. I was hurt.
I swore I would never again be so slighted.
My revenge would scare mankind forever.

'Now hear the end of the story. This fine pair,
Worn out with their wanderings, in a deep wood
Found a temple
Built long since for Cybele, Mother of the Gods,
Whose face is a black meteorite.

'Both thought they were tired enough that night
To sleep on the stone paving. Till I kissed
The ear of Hippomenes
With a whisper. As my lips touched him he shivered
Into a fit of lust like epilepsy.

'Under the temple was a cave shrine
Hollowed in solid bedrock and far older
Than the human race. An unlit crypt.
It was walled
With wooden images of the ancient gods.

'This was the sanctum doomed Hippomenes
Now defiled,
Sating himself on the body of Atalanta.
The desecrated wooden images
Averted their carved faces in horror.

'And the tower-crowned Mother of All, Cybele,
Considered plunging both
As they copulated
Into Styx, the tarpit of bubbling hell.
But that seemed insufficient to her.

'Instead, she dropped maned hides
Over their sweating backs. Hardened and hooked
Their clutching fingers into talons. Let
Their panting chest-keels deepen. Let them sweep
The dust with long tails. Gargoyle-faced,

'And now with speech to match, these godless lovers
Rumble snarls, or cough, or grunt, or roar,
They have the thorny scrub for a nuptial chamber
And are lions—their loathsome fangs obedient
Only to the bridle-bits of Cybele.

'O dear love,
These and the others like them, that disdain
To give your hounds a run but come out looking for the hunter,
For my sake, O dear boy, let them lie.
Do not ruin our love with your recklessness.'

Her lesson done, the Goddess climbed with her swans
Towards lit clouds. Meanwhile, as Adonis
Pondered her parable to find a meaning,

His hounds woke a wild boar in a wallow.
When this thug burst out, his boar-spear's point
Glanced off the bone into the hump of muscle.

The boar deftly hooked the futile weapon
Out of the wound and turned on the hunter,
Overtook the boy's panic stumble,

Stabbed its dagger tusks in under his crotch
Then ploughed him with all its fury as if unearthing
A tough tree's roots, till it tossed him aside broken.

Venus, afloat on swansdown in the high blue,
Still far short of Paphos, felt the shock-wave
Of the death-agony of Adonis.

She banked and diving steeply down through cirrus
Sighted her darling boy where he sprawled
Wallowing in a mire of gluey scarlet.

She leapt to the earth, ripping her garment open.
She clawed her hair and tore her breasts with her nails,
Pressing her wounds to his wounds as she clasped him

And screaming at the Fates: 'You hags shall not
Have it all your way. O Adonis,
Your monument shall stand as long as the sun.

'The circling year itself shall be your mourner.
Your blood shall bloom immortal in a flower.
Persephone preserved a girl's life

'And fragrance in pale mint. I shall not do less.'
Over the mangled Adonis she now dripped nectar.
His blood began to seethe—as bubbles richly

Bulge out of hot mud. Within the hour
Where he had lain a flower stood—bright-blooded
As those beads crammed in the hard rind

Of a pomegranate. This flower's life is brief.
Its petals cling so weakly, so ready to loosen
Under the first light wind that kisses it,

We call it 'windflower'.

A Flowering

MICHAEL LONGLEY

Now that my body grows woman-like I look at men
As two or three women have looked at me, then hide
Among Ovid's lovely casualties—all that blood
Colouring the grass and changing into flowers, purple,
Lily-shaped, wild hyacinth upon whose petals
We doodled our lugubrious initials, they and I,
Blood dosed with honey, tumescent, effervescent
—Clean bubbles in yellow mud—creating in an hour
My own son's beauty, the truthfulness of my nipples,
Petals that will not last long, that hang on and no more,
Youth and its flower named after the wind, anemone.

In Phrygia, Birthplace of Embroidery

LES MURRAY

When Midas, no less deserving of mercy or better for
being a king dope, had lost all faith in the gods,
either they or their haughty absence sent him metaphor,

an ever-commencing order that can resemble a philosophy
but is more charming faster, like a bird that stars into flight,
like rhyme, its junior, like edgings of the clinker-built sea—

The gold was a symbol, like a need to prize things. I'm smarter
now! he cried. I'm enlightened, as befits a great king!
My silver age will not seize the taramosalata!

But his court worked like stuff he'd learned through nonhuman ears
and like a gold effigy entitled The Hug his first daughter
stood in the strongroom. Age was like age, tears like tears,

his palace equalled his design for it, and looked no nobler tiled,
his desire for slave girls was like when he could slake it,
his wife was like an aged queen, and his heir like a child.

Mrs Midas

CAROL ANN DUFFY

It was late September. I'd just poured a glass of wine, begun
to unwind, while the vegetables cooked. The kitchen
filled with the smell of itself, relaxed, its steamy breath
gently blanching the windows. So I opened one,
then with my fingers wiped the other's glass like a brow.
He was standing under the pear tree snapping a twig.

Now the garden was long and the visibility poor, the way
the dark of the ground seems to drink the light of the sky,
but that twig in his hand was gold. And then he plucked
a pear from a branch, we grew Fondante d'Automne,
and it sat in his palm like a lightbulb. On.
I thought to myself, Is he putting fairy-lights in the tree?

He came into the house. The doorknobs gleamed.
He drew the blinds. You know the Mind; I thought of
the Field of the Cloth of Gold and of Miss Macready.
He sat in that chair like a king on a burnished throne.
The look on his face was strange, wild, vain; I said,
What in the name of God is going on? He started to laugh.

I served up the meal. For starters, corn on the cob.
Within seconds he was spitting out the teeth of the rich.
He toyed with his spoon, then mine, then with the knives, the forks.
He asked where was the wine. I poured with a shaking hand,
a fragrant, bone-dry white from Italy, then watched
as he picked up the glass, goblet, golden chalice, drank.

It was then that I started to scream. He sank to his knees.
After we'd both calmed down, I finished the wine
on my own, hearing him out. I made him sit
on the other side of the room and keep his hands to himself.

I locked the cat in the cellar. I moved the phone.
The toilet I didn't mind. I couldn't believe my ears:

how he'd had a wish. Look, we all have wishes; granted.
But who has wishes granted? Him. Do you know about gold?
It feeds no one; aurum, soft, untarnishable; slakes
no thirst. He tried to light a cigarette; I gazed, entranced,
as the blue flame played on its luteous stem. At least,
I said, you'll be able to give up smoking for good.

Separate beds. In fact, I put a chair against my door,
near petrified. He was below, turning the spare room
into the tomb of Tutankhamun. You see, we were passionate then,
in those halcyon days. Unwrapping each other, rapidly,
like presents, fast food. But now I feared his honeyed embrace,
the kiss that would turn my lips to a work of art.

And who, when it comes to the crunch, can live
with a heart of gold? That night, I dreamt I bore
his child, its perfect ore limbs, its little tongue
like a precious latch, its amber eyes
holding their pupils like flies. My dream-milk
burned in my breasts. I woke to the streaming sun.

So he had to move out. We'd a caravan
in the wilds, in a glade of its own. I drove him up
under cover of dark. He sat in the back.
And then I came home, the woman who married the fool
who wished for gold. At first I visited, odd times,
parking the car a good way off, then walking.

You knew you were getting close. Golden trout
on the grass. One day, a hare hung from a larch,
a beautiful lemon mistake. And then his footprints,
glistening next to the river's path. He was thin,
delirious; hearing, he said, the music of Pan
from the woods. Listen. That was the last straw.

What gets me now is not the idiocy or greed
but lack of thought for me. Pure selfishness. I sold
the contents of the house and came down here.
I think of him in certain lights, dawn, late afternoon,
and once a bowl of apples stopped me dead. I miss most,
even now, his hands, his warm hands on my skin, his touch.

Peleus and Thetis

JO SHAPCOTT

The bay has spread its arms wide to the sea
showing the shifting sand under clear water.
The shore's immaculate, no seaweed
rots along its edge, no prints spoil the ground.
Thetis liked to arrive here as she pleased:
    mother-naked, riding on a dolphin,
swimming and seeming like one, skin to skin.
Thetis transformed herself and laughed to feel
the surge of other shapes beneath her skin.
'My name is Thetis Creatrix,' she yelled
as she jumped ashore and ran inland towards
a stand of berry-covered myrtle trees.
At its heart there was a cave, dug out
by art or nature, no one seems to know,
though there's something of the living hand about it.
Peleus found Thetis there sound asleep.
She woke up fast, outraged to find his hands
upon her body. Not ready to give up,
Peleus clasped both arms around her neck
and tried his best to rape her on the spot.
Suddenly he found himself embracing
a large bird (but he held on to that bird).
Next she turned herself into an oak;
he wrapped his arms around the trunk, clung on,
turning his face to the side against the bark.
Her third shape was a large and spotted tigress
whose low tremendous purrs were crystal-clear:
a language to tell the pleasure of such power.
Peleus loosed his grip and ran away.
He wound up on the shore pouring good wine
over the waves, praying to the sea-gods for help
with entrails, incense, everything, until the voice

of Proteus—part poet, prophet, priest—
bellowed from the middle of his whirlpool.
'Peleus, boy, there is a way to get her:
when Thetis falls asleep in her rocky cave
truss her tightly with strong ropes and nooses
but take no notice of her fake disguises,
and don't let go whatever she tries on.'
Then Proteus pushed his face into the sea
and let the water flood over his last words.
The sun was sinking, inclining to the ocean
when Thetis came back to her stony cave.
She'd just begun to rest when Peleus
burst in and grabbed her hard but couldn't scare her.
She stretched her limbs out for the transformation,
feeling the full excitement of the art
as the image of a variegated lizard
came into her mind. Meanwhile he bound her.
While she extended her neck, lengthened her fingers,
pushed down her toes to find the form, he wrapped
the ropes around her tightly, pinning her down.
Her back began to undulate, the skin
to gleam but still the ropes held firm the human shape.
They bit into her skin, now raw and bleeding.
Excited by his strength Peleus hit out.
He gripped her throat and tore his way into her
and, smelling blood, he rubbed it on his body.
Through swollen eyelids Thetis could just see
over his shoulder the sea-god's long shadow.
'I am Thetis and I want to die,' she said.
The fruit of Peleus' rape was brave Achilles.

Aesacus, the Diver

MARK RUDMAN

His birth was a mystery.
Spoiled by the shady groves

in the mountain heights,
young Aesacus ranged the hills.

His conditions of happiness
were simple, in theory:

life in the open air; contempt
of ambition; the love of one woman

to people his solitude.
Often on his rounds he saw

Hesperie, the river-god's
daughter, but when

he caught her alone, off-guard,
drying her hair in the sun,

still wet, still clinging
to reverie, he gaped:

his gaze intent, his lust feral—
(as once, upon arriving in London

in the drought of mid-July, I had no sooner
set my bags down on the luggage rack

than I saw a woman across the running
pinks and greys of the roofs and walls—

handsome, short-cropped chestnut hair—
walk to her window

and with a sleepwalker's unswerving, even tread,
hook her thumbs under the hemline of her nightgown

and pull it over her head).
She sensed his presence

and when she zoomed in on his face
in the stark light-dark of the leaves

she panicked—crashed through thickets
to the barely travelled road

where a driver hit his brakes—too late.
Aesacus held her mangled body in his arms

and keened his lament; how could one
outburst of irrevocable lust—

which shocked him as much as her—
poison their lives forever?

(Her reaction puzzled me—
I hadn't volunteered

to wash the remaining sand off her body
to make sure no glass had wedged its way

into the calluses on her feet
on her earlier crossings of the jetty—

she'd *volunteered* to give me a 'tour'
of the musty shower room where the four

dancers hung their leotards
before they stepped into the stall;

but when I put my arms around her waist,
loosely, the way her mosaic-patterned sash was tied,

she held her body taut, her cheekbones tight.
I was so taken with the angles of her face

with her hair pulled back like that
I didn't care if she wanted to kiss me or kill me.

And though my gaze made her uneasy
she would have been angry if I had never called.)

He ran toward the high cliff,
worn thin at the base by rasping waves,

and made a running jump, as if
to free her with his own ruin.

No one cuts a more ludicrous figure
than a failed suicide.

But it wasn't his fault:
the reclusive Tethys

caught sight of the passionate
youth flailing the air and—

in a fit of misplaced compassion
for the wild boy's bad luck—

stuck a life-jacket on his back,
so as he strove to reach the bottom

and stay below, his heartbeat easing
to the rate of dolphins and whales, each stroke

bringing him closer to the giddiness
before asphyxiation, he felt himself drawn

upwards, spewed
into the ambiguous charity of light.

Again and again,
he dashed his body into the sea

but each time, however deeply
he thrust himself downwards,

he was restrained, held back
by the vest attached to his scapula—

like the wings of his own
desire . . .

It's hard to die when something
stronger than death holds you to life.

Many who found their way to that sparse rockface
mistook the diver for a cormorant;

and in time, he came to be known as—
The One Who Struggled to Stay Below the Waves.

Hecuba

CIARAN CARSON

They'd anchored off the coast of Thrace, Agamemnon and
        the comrades, waiting
For a calm; when suddenly, Achilles' ghost appears from
        nowhere, looking large
As life and twice as natural. Blood-shot glinting in his
        eye, he says,
'Forgetful of me, are you? Think my fame was buried with
        me? No, you'll have to pay
Your dues. Take you Polyxena, and put her through the usual
        rites of sacrifice. Her blood
Will be the mark of your respect.' The comrades looked
        at one another, and in that look
Became blood brothers. They dragged Polyxena from Hecuba,
        her mother.

They bring her to the altar. With sword unscabbarded,
        the priest is waiting
Then, 'Take off your hands from me,' she says,
        and rips her bodice. Shows
Her throat. Her breast. 'I'll go as someone free. It's not
        my death that grieves me,
But my mother's life. And when she comes to claim my
        body, give it to her
Freely. Don't ask for gold as ransom for this corpse.
        Exchange it for her tears.'
And then she's stabbed and stabbed again, and still her
        last gasp shows no sign of fear.
The Trojan women keened her then, and all the other dead ones
        in the house of Hecuba and Priam.

Here's Hecuba: she stuck her lips to the flapping lips
        of the wound and sucked the blood.

Her hair was slabbered and bedraggled with it. Her salt
        tears watered it.
She clawed and scrabbed herself. Then 'Daughter, last of
        all my pain, for what
Remains?'—I stare into your wound and see my wound, my
        children slaughtered.
Achilles did your brothers in, and you, and emptied me.
        His very ghost
Abuses me. I who was queen. I was someone. Look at me.
        I'm nothing now. I spin my wool
As conversation-piece for that Penelope, who sniggers,
        "*That* was Hector's mother. *That* was Priam's wife."

'And can I be alive? How can I be? O Gods, have you
        reserved some more for me?
New funerals? New death? And who would think that Priam
        would be
Happy? Happy man is he in being dead. And will my daughter
        have a gorgeous funeral?
Pomp and ceremony? Not she. She's planted in this foreign
        heap of sand.
No, wait, no, stay—there's more. There's still my
        lovely imp,
My little Polydorus. He's alive. He'll keep me. Look after
        me. What *am* I at? I haven't washed
Her wound yet. Her bloodied face. Her wound. I'll get
        some water from the shore.'

Salt water: when she got there, what was there? She shut
        her eyes. She howled.
For what was there, was Polydorus, dead. His wounds stared
        at her. The eyes of
The wounds. Their sockets. The emptiness of wounds. She
        petrified herself.
Her stony eyes grazed the ground. The sky. The ground
        again. The sky. And then
She opened sight itself and looked at him. His face. His
        eyes. His hands. His feet. All over.

And then it struck her. Polymestor. King of Thrace. He
        had to be behind it.
Polymestor. I'll show him who was queen. Who is. I am.
        I'll be. I'll get him yet.

She's like a lioness, robbed of her cubs, who crouches,
        shivers, creeps in for the kill.
She howled again. Shook her bedraggled hair. Set out for
        him, and gained an interview.
Said she had some gold, she'd kept for Polydorus. That
        she'd give him,
Polymestor, for to keep in trust. Stashed away somewhere.
        He went with her. Yes. He'd give it
To her imp. Her latest son. He would. Then she got him
        in the secret place.
Oh yes. She got him rightly. Oh. Her claws tore out
        his eyes. And then her fingernails
Went in again. Not for his eyes. What eyes? He had no eyes.
        She plucked the dark from out of the sockets.

And that was that. She got down on all fours and crawled.
        Shivered her haunches.
Growled. It's over. I have done my time. My time is done.
        What now? What
Will I be? Her jaw distended. Her arms and legs became
        all legs, and claws
Sprang from her toenails. Her bedraggled wiry coat was
        mired with blood.
There was this stone. She ran at it and gnarred at it
        and worried it.
She gawped her mouth to speak, and barked. She tossed
        the stone up
In the air. Her tongue lolled out. She barked and barked
        again, and gowls eternally around the Hellespont.

Aurora and Memnon

CIARAN CARSON

When Aurora heard about the fate of Hecuba, she didn't
        care.
She'd troubles of her own. Her own son Memnon, transfixed
        by Achilles'
Spear. He's set upon the pyre. They're going to burn him.
        She offers up a prayer
    To Jove: commemorate him in some memorable way. The god
        nods, and says, well, yes.

Memnon's bonfire then collapsed in red and black, the
        charred beams hissed and flickered.
Greasy-thick smoke sputtered up and smutched Aurora's
Sky of rose and pearl. Soot and cinders flocked together
        in a bird-shaped aura
That becomes a bird. Like an opening fist, it creaks its
        wings. Squawks and flutters.

And then the squab engendered other birds innumerable.
        They wheeled
In pyrotechnics round the pyre. The Stukas, on the third
        approach, split
In two like Prods and Taigs. Scrabbed and pecked at one
        another. Soot-flecks. Whirl-
Wind. Celtic loops and spirals chawed each other, fell
        down dead and splayed.

And every year from then to this, the Remember Memnon birds
        come back to re-enact
Their civil war. They revel in it, burning out each other.
        And that's a fact.

Acis, Galatea, Polyphemus

JAMIE MCKENDRICK

I think of the sheer foulness of Polyphemus
and then of the face of Acis which seems
unfair, it's so flawless. I lay all day
in his arms on a high green sheltered ledge
hidden from the Cyclops, that one horrid eye
molten with inflammation and fixated
    on my image. I hate to think of my image
pinned down in each of his pitifully few
brain cells like a doll-madonna stuck
in some wall shrine lit by a grey-pink bulb
on an alley of rats and gore and filth.
His outside's bad enough—hard ulcerated
slime a loathsome cindery mauve, his one eye
like an anus, a blob, a fronded jellyfish.
Then we heard him coming and watched him squat
on a jagged promontory, the waves matting
the pelt on his calves. He sets down that stick
tall as a ship's mast and starts puffing
at a pipe of giant reeds like a church organ.
I remember his song which went like this:

'O Galatea, tiny-featured as a chaffinch,
supple and slender as a rowan sapling,
smooth as Greek yoghurt, as jasper beads,
silkier than the inside of an oyster
—like a secret tree in the middle of the wood
casting a violet shadow. Your breasts are
like new-made planets in the night sky
which make the stars drop from the firmament
to cluster round your feet like leaves on fire
—you fit so exactly into your skin
your small chiselled joints must be transparent . . .'

I'll spare you some salacious details
of how he spied me bathing naked
—my breasts like bells of flesh, my nipples
parting the water . . . his voice all thick and hectic
though bits of his song weren't actually so bad.
That's why I remember it. I wouldn't mind
Acis pirating a few of those lines
but he more than makes up for that lack
with the lines of his profile—even his wrists,
even his callused heels are aphrodisiac
though his phrasing leaves something to be desired.
Cyclops then roughened his song with a lot of reproaches:

'But, O Galatea, you're harder-hearted than gnarled oak,
falser than water, more slippery than ice,
vainer than peacocks and colder than the winter sea.
Worst of all and what I hate the most are
your sudden turns of speed in spurning me.
I'd bask in your other faults if I could just
once grab hold of you. Then see if you'd escape.
And think of all the things you're missing by not
being mine: all this mountainside, that plain
as far as those squalid dinky coast resorts
that spoil the view—I'll paste them with a layer
of mud and ash as soon as I feel myself again.
Think of the orchards bowed down with pears,
pale grapes and also black ones; my caves
uncannily tuned to body-heat no matter
what season's abroad, dog days or Arctic blasts;
woodland fruits beside freshwater streams,
clumps of white-domed mushrooms, tall forests
of chestnuts, flocks of goats whose udders drip
with finest milk from which I make
clean curds by adding rennet. Are you mad?
Can't you see what I'm offering? I won't dull
your eyes with presents from the corner shop,
chocolates and daffodils—no diamanté jewels
like that cheapskate Acis gets to pin on you.

I'd dig rare gems out of the mountainside
with strange faults of fire like constellations
and fashion a necklace of dragonflies
and teach two tame owls to sing for you;
I'd twist curious lamps out of raw iron
to light you down the corridors of cave
to a bed of hoopoe crests where you would wait
for me to appear, my face dark with desire . . .
but you hate my face—it makes you cringe away.
So who says I'm that gruesome? I saw myself
in a blue pool today and thought—just look
at the size of him will you? Even Jove
who doesn't exist could never be bigger.
Does being hairy have to mean I'm vile?
Would you want a bald hound or horse, or a bird
without feathers? And if it's my one eye,
my uncompanioned eye, that bugs you what about
the sun? Two of them up there and we'd be flayed.
My eye grows on a single stem and follows
only you with its one shaft of devotion.
As for the muck on me, the stink, I'll scrub
myself with pumice every night before
we touch. Every night to touch you! O
Galatea, drop that skinny runt of an Acis
or let me at him and I'll tear his limbs
off his hairless trunk and fry them in Etna
whose channels of sulphur and blue fire
are coursing through my veins for love of you.
A love that scalds me and stops me working.
Take a look at my neglected flock. Entire fleets
pass by unscathed as if I were a lighthouse.
I just forget to wreck them. My whole life
is in arrears, in ruins like a great city
turned to burnt earth and swamps and column stumps
while all you do is quiver with disgust
at my offers and take to your exquisite heels
before I can quieten down my heartbeat

enough to speak let alone find the right words,
soft words, to let me creep closer . . .'

Raucous
and needled by his own song, he stood up
and happened to spy us—the tongue of Acis
making waves through me without the use of words
when the rocks trembled with the Cyclops's cry,
'That's the last you'll ever taste of love.'
I dived in the bay but my poor Acis
still crouched in a daze, he couldn't move as
Cyclops hefted up a rock and hurled it
crushing him, its edge alone sufficient
to flatten him. Blood trickled out from under
like autumn streams dyed coppery with leaf-juice
and the dense mass of rock, as though through guilt,
cracked open and a tall green reed sprang up
and waters gushed through the hollow rock
and a new youth waded out mid-stream,
his temples crowned in a wreath of rushes,
the waters round him whispering his name.

Circe

VICKI FEAVER

No one had a heart more susceptible to love

XIV

Because he wouldn't enter me
I made her unenterable—Scylla,
the nymph who fled from the god
whose spawn and thrashing fish tail
I wanted. I spilled my powders
into the pool where she waded
to cool herself in the gauzy
noon heat—stayed to see her crotch
grow teeth, to watch her run
from her own legs.

My father is the fiery sun.
Why do I fall for cold men?
Picus, so beautiful
on his lathered horse
I couldn't move for burning.
I covered the moon, the stars,
even my father's furnace face
with the wet sponges of clouds,
conjured a boar from the air
for him to hunt, caught up with him
in a thicket, both of us gasping.
I thought he'd lick the sweat
from my small brown breasts
like the men in Venus's stories.
When I saw he was ready for flight
I gave him feathers.

I frighten men. Even Ulysses
I had to bargain with: a year in my bed
to set his friends upright again,
unglue their trotters.
I stretched nights into weeks—
lived in the damp, ripe, gooseberry rot
of my sheets, feeding my wanderer warrior
on jellies and syrups
to help him keep up with a goddess.
In the end, it was me who sent him away.
It made me too sad: hearing
my name on his tongue
like the hiss of a tide withdrawing.

Picus

STEPHEN ROMER

So Odysseus was penned up with Circe
when a girl of hers came up: 'Macareus,
   I'll tell you a story: you see that statue,
the white one, with the bird on its head?
   That was Picus, son of Saturn—
the very image of the man, but the man
   was truer, a king too, and good to look at—
all virility, and warhorse mad,
   but just a boy, wet behind the ears,
and loutish with it, as you shall hear.
   A heartbreaker on horseback,
when he showed his face the dryads
   sighed in their trees, the nymphs
thirsted in their fountains,
   and in their riverbeds the naiads
bucked the restless torrent of their bodies.
   Picus rode roughshod over all
but one. This was Canens, a girl who sang.
   A beautiful face, to be sure, but a voice
more gifted still, an Orpheus of a girl
   moving rocks and trees, taming beasts,
stopping birds in flight—they say
   she was born of Janus by Venilia . . .
Anyway, she was barely nubile
   when cocksure Picus married her.

Riding out to hunt his wild boar
   Picus seemed to have it all,
the girl who sang (her heightened treble
   rang in his excited ears),
a stableful of thoroughbreds, a kingly seat—
   he was the living model

of bronze or marble horsemanship.
    Gathered at his neck with gold,
a purple cloak; in his fist a spear.

    Now Circe my mistress
        happened to be near,
    a singular trespasser
        on the king's rich hills
    knee-deep in grasses
        absorbed among herbs—
    when she saw through the leaves
        that heart-stopping man—
    desire came arrowing
        instantly after:
    dropping her drugs
        the sun's own daughter
    knew only one thing—
        there and then
    she must unhorse and have him.

    She left her cover
        and walked towards him
    but Picus never saw
        the trim-coifed stranger
    holding out her hands,
        too busy with his horse
    and his red-necked acolytes.
        Pique already
    mixing with desire
        the line of cruelty
    twitching at her mouth
        my mistress drew upon
    her magical self
        and swore to have him
    though he ride the wind.

Circe the susceptible, the easily inflamed,
    went to work with witchcraft, and Hecate's charms—

her thrice nine murmurings and abracadabra
    sent clouds across the sun, and thick white mist,
like steam from a spigot, snaked up every trail,
    and the whole sky was darkened by her song.
Across the tunnel vision of the king
    she sent the simulacrum of a boar
darting into some tangled undergrowth,
    and he, as she intended, went crashing after,
on foot, defenceless, hidden from his friends.
    The trap sprung, and the time ripe,
Circe spoke to him through the mist:

    'Do not despise me, or my love,
        or let disgust or principle
    destroy the spontaneity
        of two extraordinary people;
    I am a goddess, daughter of the sun,
        you are a man with godlike eyes:
    we are not incompatible—
        will you take me as I am?'

King Picus was indignant:
    'Whoever you are, the answer is *never*.
I'm a married man, and I love my wife.
    Why should I leave her for a cheap affair?
So help me God, I am hers forever!'

Now that was asking for it—
    my mistress swore that he would pay.
To scorn a goddess, and a woman!
    Hell hath no fury—as they say.
She acted in a trice, turning
    twice to the west, twice to the east,
and tapped him with her wand, thrice, like this,
    and spoke her spells above him, thrice.

At that, Sir Rectitude showed his heels,
    running like the wind, to his surprise,

which turned to outrage when he saw
    the two wings sprouting from his sides.
His purple cloak had turned to feathers
    with a golden circlet at the neck.
His eye shrank up to a beady glare,
    a single, angry, unblinking stare.
And through the woods of Latium
    flew a new bird with a hard beak
that pecked as if in pique
    on the tender bark of the king's trees—
the flight undulating, the call distinctive:
    kykykyKYUK! kykyKYUK!

Satisfied, my mistress Circe
    briskly cleared the weather;
the sun her father shone upon her
    equably as before.

But not for long. Erebus erupted
    when the angry gang of red-faced hunters
found the goddess, and dared accuse her
    of the wrong, and closed on her with spears.
Circe spat like a cat, howled like a wolf
    for Hecate and Havoc, and the freaks of night;
she shot out poisons like a rattlesnake.
    A rushing pestilence swarmed the wood,
a blizzard of ash that whitened the trees
    as if Avernus had come to light, or the living
had stumbled into it; creatures scuttled past their shins
    or caught in their hair; there were gouts of blood
on the poisoned grass, and underfoot the ground
    came alive with slimy things, the pullulation
under a lifted stone; and everywhere
    noise, screamings and whinings like shellfire,
pig-squeal and dog-bark. Groggy with horror,
    open-mouthed and stary-eyed, the hunters grew snouts
and bristles, and took on every bestial shape

as Circe set about them with her wand.
Not a solitary man escaped.

But what of Canens
      poor red-eyed Canens?
She wept her loss
      and ran distraught
six days and nights
      through Latium fields.
Further and further
      she wailed her loss
a sleepwalker wandering
      up hill, down valley,
and came at last
      to Tiber's side.
There she lay down
      and like a dying swan
sang her last song
      and wept herself away
into air and water.
      Pious souls
still name the place
      in memory of Canens,
the girl who sang.'

The Cercopes

CHARLES SIMIC

For once the father of the gods, thoroughly disgusted
By the deceitful, Bible-banging Cercopes,
And their murderous ways, wanted to change them
Into screeching monkeys, but hesitated,
    Grew uncertain, considered jackals instead,
Clucking hens, thinking perhaps a greasy rat
On the kitchen wall would suit the loudmouths better,
In fact; going from A to Z in the Bestiary
Without finding a single species to even approximate
The thieving sneaks with their lying tongues,
Not even among the shithouse flies and graveyard worms
Who are far more truthful and noble,
Make no mistake, in their conduct and in their grit.

Olive Tree

JAMES LASDUN

There already in the ploughlined
Face and brow, the knuckles'
Mud-blackened whorls, thin glinting eyes,
There in the goitred, squat, senescent frame,
Blunt lecherous hands made many in frantic groping,
There already the tree his flesh became—

Old Adam, Apulian peasant
Who chased the nymphs through the garden
Till they turned on him and in their sudden
Unbluffed glances he felt an era ending
And withered into its epitaph—
Splayed feet anchoring

An old malevolence
Once and for all in history; sinews
Packed in woodgrain; inconsolable grief
Of a failing species
Croaking from his throat in bitter berries;
Every wink of his eye a little leaf.

Phoenix

MICHAEL LONGLEY

I'll hand to you six duck eggs Orla Murphy gave me
In a beechwood bowl Ted O'Driscoll turned, a nest
Jiggling eggs from Baltimore to Belfast, from friends
You haven't met, a double-yolk inside each shell
Laid by a duck that renovates and begets itself
Inside my head as the phoenix, without grass or corn,
On a strict diet of frankincense and cardamoms,
After five centuries builds with talons and clean beak
In the top branches of a quivering palm his nest,
Lining it with cassia, spikes of nard, cinnamon chips
And yellow myrrh, brooding among the spicy smells
His own death and giving birth to an only child
Who grows up to carry through thin air the heavy nest
—His cradle, his father's coffin—to the sun's city,
In front of the sun's doorway putting his bundle down
As I shall put down the eggs Orla Murphy gave me
In a beechwood bowl Ted O'Driscoll turned for her.

According to Pythagoras

MICHAEL LONGLEY

When in good time corpses go off and ooze in the heat
Creepy-crawlies breed in them. Bury your prize bull
(A well-known experiment)—and from the putrid guts
Swarm flower-crazy bees, industrious country-types
Working hard, as did their host, with harvest in mind.
An interred warhorse produces hornets. Remove
A shore-crab's hollow claw, lay it to rest: the result
Is a scorpion charging with its tail bent like a hook.
Worms cosy in cocoons of white thread grow into
Butterflies, souls of the dead. Any farmer knows that.

Germs in mud generate green frogs: legless at first
They soon sprout swimming and jumping equipment.
A she-bear's cub is a lump of meat whose stumpy
Non-legs she licks into shape in her own image.
The honey-bees' larvae born in those waxy hexagons
Only get feet and wings later on. That's obvious.
Think of peacocks, eagles, doves, the bird family
As a whole, all starting inside eggs: hard to believe.
There's a theory that in the grave the backbone rots
Away and the spinal cord turns into a snake.

The fundamental interconnectedness of all things
Is incredible enough, but did you know that
Hyenas change sex? The female mounted by a male
Just minutes before becomes a male herself. Then
There's the chameleon that feeds off wind and air
And takes the colour of whatever it's standing on.
Air transforms lynxes' urine into stones and hardens
Coral, that softly swaying underwater plant.
I could go on and on with these scientific facts.
If it wasn't so late I'd tell you a whole lot more.

Index of Translators

Biographical Notes

Index of Translators

Biographical Notes

FLEUR ADCOCK was born in New Zealand and has lived in England since 1963. Her collections of poetry include *Selected Poems* (1983), *The Incident Book* (1986), and *Time Zones* (1991). She has also translated medieval Latin poetry and works by the modern Romanian poets Grete Tartler and Daniela Crasnaru. She is editor of *The Oxford Book of Contemporary New Zealand Poetry* and *The Faber Book of Twentieth Century Women's Poetry*.

SIMON ARMITAGE was born in 1963 and lives in Huddersfield, England. He is the author of *Zoom!* (1989), *Xanadu* (1992), *Kid* (1992), and *The Book of Matches* (1993). He edits poetry for *The Guardian* and is poetry editor at Chatto & Windus in London.

EAVAN BOLAND was born in Belfast in 1944 and was educated at Trinity College, Dublin. Her collections include *The Journey* (1987), *Selected Poems* (1989), *Outside History* (1991), and *In a Time of Violence* (1994).

CIARAN CARSON was born in Belfast in 1948, was educated at Queen's University, Belfast, and works as the Traditional Arts Officer of the Arts Council of Northern Ireland. He is the author of the collections *The New Estate* (1976), *The Irish for No* (1987), and *Belfast Confetti* (1989), which won the *Irish Times*/Aer Lingus Prize for Poetry. His most recent collection is *First Language* (1994).

AMY CLAMPITT was born and brought up in rural Iowa, and lived mainly in New York City. Her poems have been published in five full-length books, most recently *A Silence Opens* (1994). She was named a MacArthur Fellow in 1992, was a chancellor of the Academy of American Poets and a member of the American Academy of Arts and Letters, and taught at William and Mary, Amherst, and Smith. She died in September 1994.

FRED D'AGUIAR was born in London in 1961 and grew up there and in Guyana. Three collections of his poetry have been published: *Mama Dot* (1985), *Airy Hall* (1989), and *British Subjects* (1993). The novel *The Longest Memory*

(1994) is his most recent book. He is a visiting writer at Amherst College in Massachusetts.

Born in Glasgow in 1955, CAROL ANN DUFFY grew up in Staffordshire and attended university in Liverpool before moving to London. Her 1993 collection of poems, *Mean Time*, won the Whitbread Prize for Poetry and the Forward Prize. Her other collections are *Standing Female Nude*, *The Other Country*, and *Selling Manhattan*, which won the Somerset Maugham Award in 1988. She also edited an anthology for teenagers entitled *I Wouldn't Thank You for a Valentine*.

VICKI FEAVER was born in Nottingham in 1943, studied at Durham and University College, London, and now teaches at the West Sussex Institute in Chichester. She is the author of two collections of poetry: *Close Relatives* (1981) and *The Handless Maiden* (1994).

ALICE FULTON is a MacArthur Fellow, and has been a fellow of the Ingram Merrill and Guggenheim foundations. Her latest book of poetry is *Sensual Math*. Her other books are *Powers of Congress*, *Palladium*, and *Dance Script with Electric Ballerina*. She is professor of English at the University of Michigan, Ann Arbor.

JORIE GRAHAM is the author of five books of poetry. Her most recent is *Materialism* (1992). She teaches at the University of Iowa.

THOM GUNN, born in England in 1929, moved to California in 1954 and lives in San Francisco. His most recent books are *The Man with Night Sweats* (1992), *Shelf Life* (prose, 1993), and *Collected Poems* (1994).

SEAMUS HEANEY was born in County Derry, Northern Ireland. Now a resident of Dublin, he spends half of each year teaching at Harvard University. He is a member of the Irish Academy of Letters and has been the recipient of many honors and awards for his poetry.

MICHAEL HOFMANN's books of poetry are *Nights in the Iron Hotel*, *Acrimony*, and *Corona, Corona*. He has translated more than a dozen books from the German, including works by Bertolt Brecht and Franz Kafka. He writes criticism for *The Times* of London and the *London Review of Books*, and lives in London.

TED HUGHES was born in 1930 and has been the Poet Laureate to Queen Elizabeth II since 1984. His most recent books are *Wolfwatching* (1989), a book of poems; *Shakespeare and the Goddess of Complete Being* (1992), a study of Shakespeare's dramatic equation; *The Iron Woman* (1993), a story for children; and *Winter Pollen* (1994), a collection of essays. He lives in Devon.

LAWRENCE JOSEPH is the author of three books of poetry: *Before Our Eyes* (1993), *Curriculum Vitae* (1988), and *Shouting at No One* (1983). He lives in New York City, where he is professor of law at St. John's University School of Law.

KARL KIRCHWEY's books of poetry are *A Wandering Island* (1990) and *Those I Guard* (1993). He has received Ingram Merrill and Guggenheim fellowships and the Rome Prize in Literature. He is the director of the Unterberg Poetry Center of the 92nd Street YM-YWHA in New York City.

KENNETH KOCH's most recent books are *One Train* (new poems) and *On the Great Atlantic Railway* (selected poems), both published in 1994; *Hotel Lambosa* (short stories, 1993); and a British *Selected Poems* (1991). He teaches at Columbia University and lives in New York City.

JAMES LASDUN was born in London and now lives in the United States, where he teaches at Sarah Lawrence College. Two collections of his short stories and one of his poetry have been published. His work has appeared in the *London Review of Books*, *The New Yorker*, *The Times Literary Supplement*, *The Paris Review*, and *Grand Street*.

WILLIAM LOGAN is the author of three books of poetry: *Sad-Faced Men*, *Difficulty*, and *Sullen Weedy Lakes*. He teaches at the University of Florida and lives in Florida and in Cambridge, England.

MICHAEL LONGLEY was born in Belfast in 1939, was educated at Trinity College, Dublin, and worked for twenty years for the Arts Council of Northern Ireland. His *Gorse Fires* won the Whitbread Prize for poetry in 1991, and his *Poems 1963–1983* was reissued the same year. His most recent collection is *The Ghost Orchid*.

J. D. MCCLATCHY is the author of three collections of poetry, a book of essays, and several libretti. He is editor of *The Yale Review*.

JAMIE MCKENDRICK was born in Liverpool in 1955. He worked for several years in southern Italy and now works in Oxford as a teacher, reviewer, and translator. He has had two books of poetry published: *The Sirocco* (1991) and *The Kiosk on the Brink* (1993).

DEREK MAHON was born in 1941 and graduated from Trinity College, Dublin, where he was later writer-in-residence. He worked for some years in London as a journalist and screenwriter and now lives in New York City and teaches at New York University. His *Selected Poems* appeared in 1991.

GLYN MAXWELL was born in 1962 in Hertfordshire, of Welsh parents. He is the author of two books of poetry, *Tale of the Mayor's Son* (1990) and *Out of the Rain* (1992), as well as a book of plays and the novel *Blue Burneau* (1994). He has won the Somerset Maugham Travel Prize and the Eric Gregory Award for poets under thirty.

PAUL MULDOON, who was born in Northern Ireland in 1951, is "generally regarded as the leading Irish poet of his generation" (*Time Out*). His chief collections of poetry are *New Weather* (1973), *Mules* (1977), *Why Brownlee Left* (1980), *Quoof* (1983), *Meeting the British* (1987), *Selected Poems 1968–86* (1987), *Madoc: A Mystery* (1990), and *The Annals of Chile* (1994).

LES MURRAY lives in his native Bunyah, New South Wales. His books include *The Rabbiter's Bounty: Collected Poems* (1991), *The Boys Who Stole the Funeral* (1991), *Dog Fox Field* (1992), and *Translations from the Natural World* (1994).

TOM PAULIN was born in Leeds in 1949 and grew up in Northern Ireland. A book of his essays, *Minotaur: Poetry and the Nation State*, was published in 1992. His latest collection of poems is *Walking a Line* (1994).

ROBERT PINSKY is professor of English and creative writing at Boston University. His most recent work is a verse translation of Dante's *Inferno*. His collections of poetry include *An Explanation of America* (1979) and *The Want Bone* (1990).

JUSTIN QUINN was born in Ireland in 1968 and was educated at Trinity College, Dublin. He lives in Prague, and his first book of poems will be published in 1995.

CRAIG RAINE is the author of three volumes of poetry: *The Onion, Memory* (1978), *A Martian Sends a Postcard Home* (1979), and *Rich* (1986). He has also published a libretto, a verse play, and a collection of essays. His most recent book is a novel in verse, *History: The Home Movie* (1994).

PETER READING was born in 1946 in Liverpool and trained as a painter at Liverpool College of Art. He has been a teacher, a lecturer in art history, a millworker, and a weighbridge operator. He is the author of nineteen volumes of verse, the most recent of which is *Last Poems* (1994).

PETER REDGROVE is the author of twenty-three books of verse and seven novels, and is well known as a dramatist. He won the Rome Prize in 1982. He has also published a manifesto on the Gaia hypothesis and a study of menstrual psychology (with Penelope Shuttle), and he is writing a study of Mesmerism.

CHRISTOPHER REID is the author of five books of poetry, most recently *In the Echoey Tunnel* (1991) and *Universes* (1994). He is poetry editor at Faber & Faber in London.

ROBIN ROBERTSON is from the northeast coast of Scotland. He now lives and works in London. Most recently, his poems have appeared in the *London Review of Books* and *The Observer*.

STEPHEN ROMER was born in England in 1957 and was educated at Cambridge and Harvard. He has lived in France since 1980 and teaches at the University of Tours. He is the author of two collections of poetry: *Idols* (1986) and *Plato's Ladder* (1992). A translator of contemporary French poetry, he writes on French literature and in 1993 edited a collection of essays on Anglo-French translation.

MARK RUDMAN was born in 1948 in New York City, where he now lives, and grew up in the Midwest and the West. He is the author of three books of poetry—*By Contraries*, *The Nowhere Steps*, and *Rider*—and of two books of prose: *Robert Lowell: Diverse Voices* and *Realm of Unknowing*.

FREDERICK SEIDEL's books of poetry are *Final Solutions*; *Sunrise*, winner of the Lamont Prize and the 1980 National Book Critics Circle Award in Poetry; *These Days*; and *My Tokyo*.

JO SHAPCOTT was born in London in 1953, was educated at Trinity College, Dublin, and at Oxford, and now lives in London. Her collections are *Electroplating the Baby* (1988) and *Phrase Book* (1992). She has held fellowships at Cambridge and Harvard universities.

CHARLES SIMIC is the author of fourteen collections of poetry, three books of prose, and numerous translations. He has won many awards, including a MacArthur Fellowship and a Pulitzer Prize. His most recent book of poems is *A Wedding in Hell* (1994).

CHARLES TOMLINSON's books of poems include his *Collected Poems* (1992), *The Door in the Wall* (1994), and *Jubilation*. In 1993 he published his translation of *The Selected Poems of Attilio Bertolucci* and received the Bennett Award of the *Hudson Review* for literary achievement.

DAVID WHEATLEY was born in Dublin in 1970. His poetry has been widely published in Britain and Ireland. He is currently a research student at Trinity College, Dublin.

C. K. WILLIAMS was born in New Jersey in 1936. He is a professor of English at George Mason University and lives part of the year in Paris. His book *Flesh and Blood* won the National Book Critics Circle Award in Poetry in 1987, and in 1988 he received the Lila Acheson Wallace / Reader's Digest Writers' Award. His *Selected Poems* recently appeared.